Dangerous Coastline 1939-1945

A wartime childhood in Birchington, Kent

by

Derek S. Hart

Edited by Jennie Burgess M.A.
2004

Published by K.H.McIntosh for
BIRCHINTON HERITAGE TRUST

Acknowledgements

Firstly, I would like to thank Maureen Hart and her two sons, Jason and Justin, for entrusting me with Derek's manuscript and lending me so many items and pictures from his collection.

I must next acknowledge my grateful thanks to all those people who have given me permission to include additional material in Derek's text :-

to the Ordnance Survey, Romsey Road, Southampton, SO16 4GU, for their generous permission to include maps originally drawn by Derek from unspecified originals;

to Froglets Publications Ltd., Brasted Chart, Westerham, Kent, TN16 1LY, for permission to include the pictures of the mine on Deal beach (p. 164), the class lesson in a shelter (p. 165) and the Blitz in Canterbury (p. 125) from "Kent at War" by Bob Ogley;

to Buckland Publications, Barwick Road, Dover CT17 0LG, for permission to include a picture of the Wellington Bomber with its degausser ring suspended beneath it (p. 18) from "To a Safer Place" by Peter Hayward;

to Simmons Aerofilms Ltd, 32-34 Station Close, Potters Bar, Herts, EN6 1TL, for permission to use part of one of their aerial photos of Birchington from 1949;

to W.H. Allen & Co. Plc., Sekforde House, 175-179 St John Street, London EC1V 4LL, whom I have tried unsuccessfully to contact, concerning a book by Peter Haining, called "Spitfire Summer". From this book I have included a photo of "Mrs. England" (p. 126) and a small picture of "Suggestion for another method of obstructing arterial roads by bars let into the surface" (p. 85). This one was included in Peter Haining's book from the "London Illustrated News" 15th June 1940 on pp. 822-3. All other photos were taken by either Derek or the editor.

Another very warm vote of thanks goes to Charlie Smart, who has painted us such a superb cover at very short notice to my rather exacting requirements!

In Derek's original manuscript he included the following acknowledgements:
"I wish to thank my daughter-in-law Amanda for the extended use of her typewriter, the Margate and Westgate-on-Sea Public Libraries for their kind assistance and to my wife Maureen for her patience while I was compiling this book."
To this I must add my own thanks to the staff of Birchington Library for their unfailing help in tracing the various books I myself needed to consult.

I must also render very grateful thanks to Kinn Mcintosh for all her help and advice in guiding me through the many pitfalls on the road to getting this book into print, and to the people who have kindly helped me to proofread the completed manuscript including Ted Tranter and Gerald Colson. Finally I would like to thank Howard Smith of Parkers printers for his patience and understanding with such a novice in this business.

ISBN 0 9544789 -2-4

The book is dedicated to Derek Hart in grateful remembrance

All profits to the Birchington Heritage Trust, through the generosity of Maureen Hart and her sons

Cover picture by Charlie Smart of Birchington

Printed and designed by E.C.Parker Ltd, Canterbury 766555

Derek Hart (left) on the occasion of his retirment, 2 November 1991, at Manston Airport with David Beck.

Introduction

Derek Hart wrote this book after he retired from the Post Office in 1991. Having attended a seminar for newly retired staff, he was attracted to the idea of writing the story of his wartime childhood. He realised that his experiences were unusual because so few of Birchington's children remained in the village during the war. When the schools closed in 1940, the majority of local children were evacuated to Staffordshire, with most of the five to eleven year-olds being billeted in the Tamworth area.

Derek went to great lengths to check the accuracy of his memories and spent many hours at local libraries and checking other sources of reference. He tried to find a publisher for his work, but none was interested at that time. Sadly, he died very suddenly on the 28th May 2003 without seeing his dream realised. His widow, Maureen, and his two sons, Jason and Justin, felt that the work was of real significance and ought, somehow, to reach a local audience, so they approached the Birchington Heritage Trust.

As soon as I began to read it I felt sure that it was of immense value to local readers, because so little information has survived from this period. Between 1940 and 1945 we only have a handful of Parish magazines, usually one of the most fruitful sources of information. The local press holds some information, but it seldom covered the ordinary day-to-day events in Birchington that Derek has so expertly captured. The manuscript has been slightly edited, but only so that it will read more easily for young and old alike. The older generation will know what all the wartime 'jargon' means, so we hope they will forgive some of what, to them, may seem like obvious explanations.

Derek's family are so pleased to see this work in print and feel it is a fitting memorial to a loving husband, father and grandfather, as well as a worthy contribution to our local knowledge of a most amazing period in our island's history, or as Churchill so aptly called it, "our finest hour".

Jennie Burgess
Parish Archivist
Birchington: November 2003

Contents

Chapter 1

1920s

Move to Minnis Bay

My parents moved to Birchington in Kent in the 1920s. My elder brother, Owen, was born in December 1929 and, needing more room than their flat in Epple Bay Road afforded them, they rented a large semi-detached house in Minnis Road. It was next door to Mrs Ward and her two daughters, none of whom were ever seen by the general public. The Ward sisters and their mother seldom ventured further than their back garden, which was surrounded by tall hedges. Local tradesmen delivered and took orders, then collected the money left on the doorstep, which was on the side of the house. They were wealthy people who had connections with Lord Carson, who lived at Cleve Court, on the outskirts of Acol.

Rats

My father noticed a lot of rats in our back garden. Knowing he had nothing to attract them, this puzzled him. One day he heard voices coming from next door and beckoned to my mother. They looked through one of the gaps in the hedge and saw the two daughters calling the rats by name and feeding them with saucers of bread and milk. It was their only contact with the outside world and so they had made pets of them. Eventually, in 1938, the police were called, because the mother had been dead in the house for several months. These events made headlines in the National Press at the time. Some local people took pity on the two sisters and took them into their home.

Our house in Ethelbert Road at Minnis Bay

Soon afterwards, the owner of our house wanted it back, not long after my parents had decorated it from top to bottom and transformed the wilderness of a garden into a beautiful one. She offered to let them rent part of the house, but they found a three-bedroomed one to rent in Ethelbert Road, Minnis Bay, just 236 yards from the sea. The front bay windows had a view of the sea to the left, while the rear windows upstairs had magnificent views across the Bay to Reculver Towers. From all the bedroom windows there was also a good view of the western end of the runway at Manston aerodrome.

The family grows

I was born on 14th November 1934 and my sister was born two years later. There was a "lane", or service road, that ran along the back of all the properties. The only way through the long grass was via a cinder track down the middle. Some of these rear lanes had been made up with tarmac and main drainage, but ours was still unmade.

One day in the mid 1930s my father was wheeling a garden barrow down the path into the lane, followed by Owen with his small barrow. While my grandmother held me up, she and my mother were watching from the kitchen window. Suddenly the ground gave way beneath my father and brother, as they disappeared into a cesspit, barrows as well. My mother, who had rushed down the path to find out what had happened, also fell down the hole, landing on top of my father. Luckily, no one was

We lived in the second house from the right, with the Ward family on left of us.

injured. They managed to get out by my mother standing on my father's shoulders. The hole was about eight feet deep. It was later filled in by the local authorities. The house we lived in was only a few years old and the roads around had not yet been made up. One day, to our delight, the workmen came to start work. For hours we watched the steamroller making its way up and down our road. During this work, Owen slipped over and fell in the newly tarred Lyell Road, so we had to go straight home for mother to clean it off with butter.

My Father

Before moving to Kent, my parents lived in Berkshire, where my father studied nursery gardening at Reading University. Here in East Kent, there was little call for such work, so he had to resort to gardening for the wealthy people, who abounded in the area, along with any other jobs that were available. At one stage he did a milk round with a horse and cart, helped by Owen. One rather irate, wealthy lady customer called him back after he had delivered her milk, stating, "This milk is more like water", to which my father replied, "Ah yes, madam, but we do use the best water" – he got the sack!

My father was one of the Old Contemptibles from W.W.I and fought at the Battle of the Somme. He had been temporarily blinded and deafened, but as soon as he was better, he was sent back to the Front again and again. He was a great lover of horses and was leading eight of them when a shell exploded among them, killing them all, including his own. A keen sportsman, he enjoyed keeping himself fit; he boxed for his regiment, the 10th Royal Hussars. When the war ended he was only expected to live a few months, but my mother gradually nursed him back to health.

He was a great philosopher, with many of his predictions coming true. He did a huge amount of reading, especially the books by the war historian Basil Liddell-Hart. To make ends meet, my mother, like so many others in Minnis Bay, took in visitors during the summer months. Living so close to the sea and Mother being a wonderful cook, we were always full up.

Trains

As a small boy, I clearly remember walking up our hallway to meet Owen when he came home from Haine Isolation Hospital, Ramsgate, after suffering from an attack of Scarlet Fever. Later on, when he was old enough, he took me to see the trains that ran nearby. That is how I became initiated into steam and we developed our ambition to become engine drivers! We could see the trains going by from our bedroom window, but we were not near enough to see the locomotive numbers – most infuriating! So we would go to the nearest spotting place by Horsa Road, where there was an occupational crossing we named "Miss Lawrence's". Miss Lawrence once had a kindergarten school in a garage right beside the railway boundary, which Owen attended at an early age.

My interest in trains has remained all my life. I took the photograph of the Golden Arrow as it came through the village in 1991.

The Golden Arrow at Birchington Station in 1991

Chapter 2

1939

Winter fun

In the winter of 1938/9 we had a lot of snow. My Aunt Maud and Uncle Ernie, with their daughter Gloria, who was the same age as Owen, came to stay with us. One snowy day while the tide was in, Owen, Gloria, my young sister and I started rolling a snowball along the promenade, till it grew to four or five feet high. By this time, it was so heavy that we could hardly move it. With one last heave, we pushed it over the edge into the sea. Little did we realise as we watched it floating along that quite soon we would witness a mine doing the same thing.

Gloria had borrowed my mother's shoes and we also took the pushchair in case my little 3 year old sister needed it. On the way home, the shoes became saturated, so Gloria took them off, then discovered she could not get them back on again. The only thing to do was sit Gloria in the pushchair, but she was ten years old and too big for it. We were doing quite well with the three of us pushing her home, when a wheel came off. That was it – Gloria had to walk back with no shoes in the deep snow, with a pair of ruined shoes and a broken pushchair. We were all in deep trouble when we eventually got home!

Local geography
(See Map 1 overleaf)

The area from Reculver Towers to Plum Pudding Island is marshland and very low-lying, standing just a few feet above sea level. Chambers Wall Farmhouse, with its walls four feet thick at the base, stands just below sea level. From Plum Pudding Island, the land along the coast gradually rises till it reaches Minnis Road. It then rises quite sharply by the Minnis Bay Hotel to Beresford Gap, which had chalk cliffs of about 35 feet in height. Here we would all explore the numerous caves, once used by smugglers. Some of these caves went inland as much as one and a half miles I believe, but we never ventured very far for fear of a chalk fall.

My father knew the gardener of one of the big houses on The Parade along the cliff top. While mowing the lawn one day, the mower disappeared through the lawn, dropping into the sea below. From our bedroom window, Owen and I could watch warships silhouetted against an orange sky, sailing along the horizon. We would then try to identify them by using our "Wills" cigarette cards.

Bedlam

It had been made public that on the 13th February an old detached house on the corner of Devon and Essex Gardens, named Bedlam, was to be set alight and used as fire practice by the local fire brigades so Mother took us along to watch. I felt it was awful to do such a thing to this nice old house which was over 400 years old. Little did we know that they would soon be fighting real fires in the not too distant future. My parents discussed the serious situation in Europe till late into the night. We would often listen, seated at the top of the stairs. They still held vivid memories of the First World War and my father predicted, "We will soon be at war with Germany – and only 21 years since the last one."

The burning of Bedlam Cottage was advertised in the local press, so large numbers of people braved the February chill to watch the spectacle.

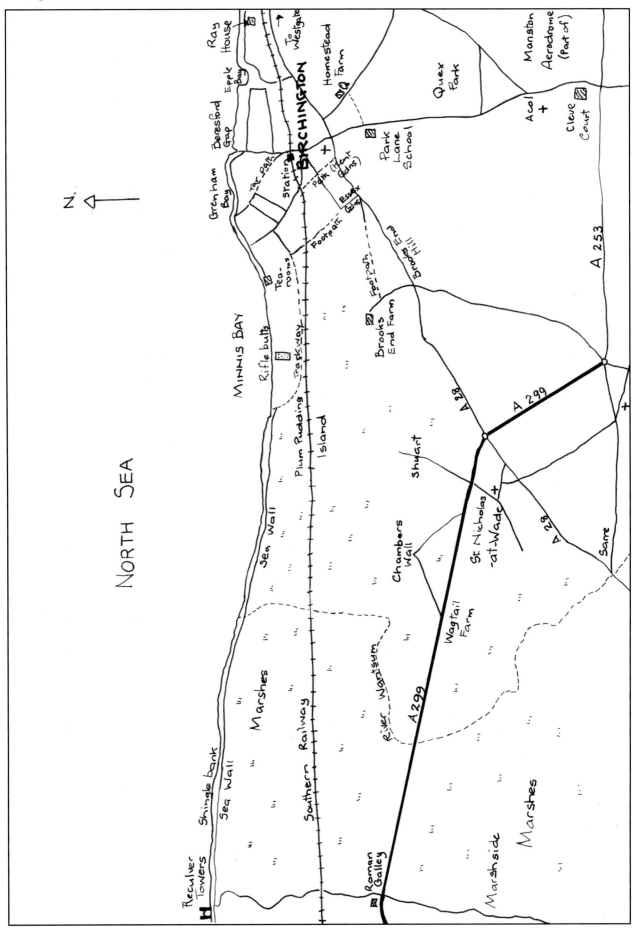

MAP 1
Map showing the marshes between Reculver and Minnis Bay

Strangers

"What about all the foreigners here in Minnis Bay – with Ribbentrop living just around the corner and that German woman just across the road?" asked my mother, who often saw them both when she went shopping in the village. The 'German woman' lived at "Creta" and used to lecture all over Britain. She helped to run a private girls' school in the Bay and was a great friend of Miss Haig, whose father had started the Congregational Church at Minnis Bay.

Up until just before the outbreak of World War II, Germany's Foreign Minister and Hitler's right-hand man for armed diplomacy, Joachim von Ribbentrop, had been staying just 300 yards from our house. He was renting the large detached bungalow called "Greenheyes" in Harold Road, just 100 yards from the cliff edge and the caves.

We did not have a wireless so my father would read out the news from the "Mirror" or the "Daily Express", as he sat at the dining room table. My mother would be listening in the adjacent kitchen. We three children had learnt of Hitler invading the countries in Europe, so we knew that it would soon be the turn of France, Belgium and Holland. "Just across the water on the other side," we often heard our parents say. By this time, we had all been issued with gas masks, ours being a little smaller than our parents'. Later on, the gas masks were fitted with a bright green extension, giving it a long snout.

War is declared

Then on the 3rd September, my father brought home an evening newspaper, sat down and read out "This morning the British Ambassador in Berlin handed the German government a final note stating that, unless we heard from them by 11 o'clock that they were prepared at once to withdraw their troops from Poland, a state of war would exist between us. I have to tell you that no such undertaking has been received, and that consequently this country is at war with Germany." For a while there was silence, then my father said, "I knew it." My mother put her arms around us children, as my father said; "Now we must all stick together." The next day my father was in the police force at R.A.F. Manston.

Gas masks

Overnight almost the whole population of Minnis Bay left – we were the only children left in the area. The Minnis Bay Hotel, situated only 50 yards from the cliff edge, along with its annex almost opposite and within 250 yards of our house, remained open. All civilians had to attend the Ritz Cinema in Station Road, Birchington, with their gas masks, to be shown how to make sure they were airtight. Everybody then had to put on their masks without help from anyone else. A gas canister was then placed on the stage and opened. A short while later we were instructed to remove our masks to see the effect of the gas, then we were ordered to put them on again.

"Greenheyes", the bungalow in Harold Road occupied by Joachim von Ribbentrop until just before the outbreak of Word War II.

Black-out

The 'blackout' came into operation immediately. Even though we had only gas and no electricity, we had to have the thick black curtains drawn before we could strike a match to light the mantle. My parents decided we should sleep downstairs, so we abandoned our bedrooms to sleep on mattresses on the floor under the huge kitchen table. The table with its two-inch thick solid wooden top and six-inch diameter legs was moved into the dining room at the back of the house. We three children were against the wall backing onto the kitchen, while my parents slept towards the fireplace end. We all felt safer downstairs, where, if necessary, we could make a quick exit to the back door via the kitchen.

First troops arrive

The first of the troops, the Hampshire Regiment, were billeted in the Minnis Bay Hotel annexe. They soon sent someone to check to see that everything in our house was in order and then instructed us to tell our parents of any strange people or occurrences in the area. They were then to tell someone in the Bay Hotel, where they usually went for a drink in the evening and where the bar was always full of troops. The soldiers wanted to know the recent and past history of the area, also any information on the few remaining residents and, most important of all, any who had left the area in great haste. They, in turn, passed on secret information for our safekeeping, along with any news not for publication in the newspapers or on the wireless. Owen, my sister and I went along to the rear of the annexe, where the soldiers gave us cap badges and shoulder flashes from their regiment. We often heard distant explosions, but could see nothing. My parents said they were mines going off far out at sea.

Battalion of troops in Statoin Road, Birchington c. 1943. The Wayside Café can be seen on the corner of Eastfield Road.

Chapter 3

1940

Early months

Early in 1940, we were supplied with an Anderson shelter, which we put up at the bottom of the garden. I felt quite grown up helping to pile earth over the shelter with my small sand spade. An air raid siren was erected on a tall post by the end shop near the Post Office Stores in Minnis Road. A test was to be made on Sunday morning. Owen got there before the allotted time that had been announced in the local Press, and put his ear to the post to find out if he could hear it. Hear It? He certainly did – and came running all the way back home, holding his hand over his ear!

Troops from the Lancashire Fusiliers moved into the large properties around us. Some of these soldiers also gave us cap badges and shoulder flashes after we watched them training. One in a hundred men had a .303 Lee-Enfield rifle, while the remainder had broom handles and wooden cut-outs of the rifles – the silhouettes of which looked authentic from afar!

Shoulder flashes given to Owen and me by the troops based at Minnis Bay during W.W. II

Dunkirk

Early in May, Germany invaded Belgium and Holland – they were now where my mother had predicted "Just across the water", and my parents looked more worried than ever. Not long after, an army officer with some ratings knocked on the front door. He asked mother if she had any spare blankets. When she asked why, he told her that some of our troops were coming back from Dunkirk, landing at Margate, Ramsgate and Dover harbours right now. Mother gave him as many as she could spare and they gratefully went on their way.

With this information, we all headed for Margate. The single-decker No: 70 bus service no longer ran to Minnis Bay, so we all hurried up the three-quarters of a mile to Birchington station and caught the Margate bus. This was stopped at the Nayland Rock Hotel, where we got off and walked the short distance to Margate railway station, where we had a good view of the harbour and jetty.

There, anchored off the jetty, were boats of all shapes and sizes, but most memorable of all was the never ending column of soldiers walking slowly to the station in silence, except for the sound of their boots on the gravel. We were used to seeing soldiers smartly turned out for training, but seeing this was an awful shock. For a while I couldn't take in that this was *our* army. A lot of them were covered in black oil. Some had their heads bandaged, others had arms in slings; some were only partly dressed, with no jackets, shirts, hats or belts. Among them we saw French soldiers, noticeable by their steel helmets. My mother got talking to someone nearby, who told her we had snatched the British Expeditionary Force from the beaches of Dunkirk.

Owen and I noticed that most of the locomotives hauling the troop trains were N. or U. class 2.6.0 Moguls, ideal for this work. Later on, under great secrecy, we learnt that many little ships had sailed past our house under cover of darkness from Sheerness to Dunkirk. A total of 338,226 soldiers were brought back to England. My father and mother were thrilled, "This is the first time that Hitler has failed – they call this the 'Miracle of Dunkirk'," my father announced.

Then all the schools closed down.

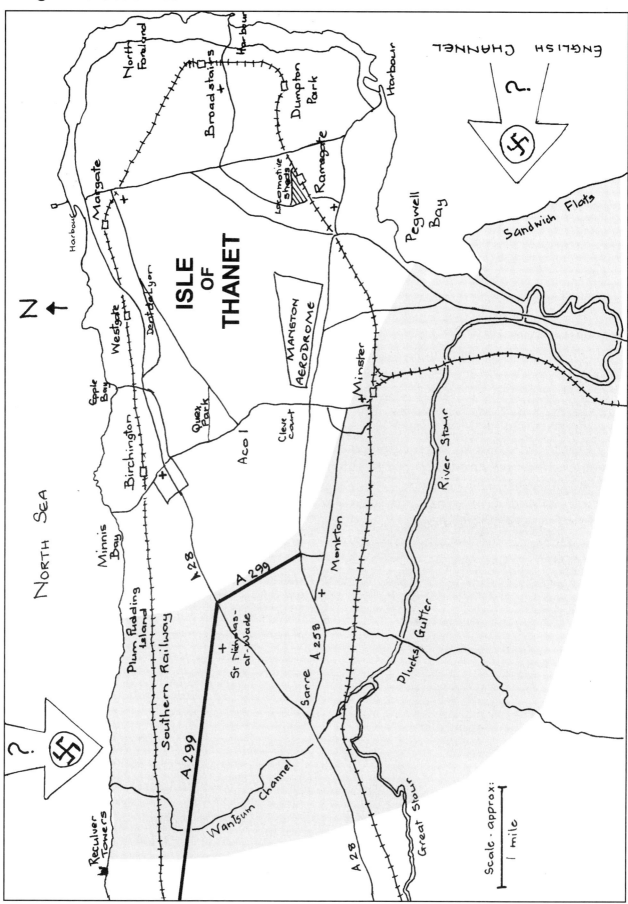

MAP 2
Map showing possible routes for a German invasion of Britain in 1940

Threat of invasion

Evacuation of the children from the area to Staffordshire was the call, but my mother insisted that if we went, she must go too. The authorities refused to allow her to accompany us, so we all stayed at home with our parents. A few days later, my father read out Winston Churchill's broadcast to the Nation, "We shall go on to the end ....". "He's bluffing, 'fight them on the beaches' – with what? We haven't got anything. If Hitler knew, he could come over and walk right in. Churchill warned them years ago that Germany was re-arming for war, but was shouted down time and again with calls of 'War-monger'." My father was livid – I had never seen him in such a rage.

Germany had been preparing for war since the early 1930s. With the rise of Hitler and the Third Reich, his plans were prepared well in advance. In England during the 1930s, the new arterial road, the A 299, known locally as the Thanet Way, was built from the A2 at Brenley Corner near Faversham to the A253 near Monkton. But British Intelligence was aware of a German architect who had engineered and devised a wide single carriageway with long, straight, flat stretches, to act as emergency runways. On the Thanet Way, there was a particular remote stretch of road, between the Roman Galley public house opposite Reculver Towers, and Wagtail Farm at St Nicholas-at-Wade, which was a mile long. After this the road rises through a quarter mile cutting. There were wide grass verges along the whole 17-mile length of the road. A second flat and open stretch lay between the junction with the A28 and the A253. There were no telegraph poles, signs, etc., along either of these stretches and the grass verges were kept short and clear. Both would make ideal landing grounds for enemy planes.
(See Map 2 opposite)

We heard from our troops that Goering's invasion plans were for the Luftwaffe to land Ju. 52 troop-carriers using these roads as landing strips. After the troops had disembarked, the planes were to take off and head towards Herne Bay, the prevailing wind being westerly, and then head back to France to re-load. With

'Road Obstructions' from a series of suggestions issued during 1940 to deter enemy aircraft from landing

utmost urgency, huge 'H' section girders were implanted at random along the grass verges and into the road itself. The same type of girders were embedded all over the beach, out past the low water mark from Reculver to Minnis Bay Hotel in the vast stretches of firm sand.

My impression of Minnis Bay with the iron girders to deter amphibious landings

Dangerous Coastline

For centuries Reculver Towers had been used as a landmark. Here was the ideal spot for a sea-borne landing area. The sea wall, built of earth in the reign of Henry VIII, was three miles long and only 10 feet high, with gradually sloping sides and a shingle top on the north seaward side and held in place with wattles. To the south were sloping grass sides, with open marshland beyond, followed by the railway line and then the Thanet Way, a distance of a mile in all. Initially, there were no gun emplacements in the vicinity, the nearest being a 2.6" one at Fort Crescent at Margate. Any Panzers that had landed would have had little or no opposition.

This area on the north coast of Thanet was once occupied by the Romans, who built a fort at Reculver at the northern opening of the Wantsum Channel, and another at the southern end called Richborough, on the Sandwich flats. The Wantsum, though much reduced in width, still divides Thanet from the Kent mainland. Although it is now silted up, it is still just navigable by canoe. It used to be almost a mile wide in places 1,500 years ago and the Romans sailed their large fleet of ships along it to avoid the rough weather around the North Foreland. To the south of Thanet, stretching from Pegwell Bay towards Sandwich are the Flats, another marshy area a few feet above sea level, with no sea wall. This, we heard, was to be the enemy's second sea-borne landing zone, simultaneously with the invasion in the north of the island.

Both were to advance four miles where they would rendezvous near Monkton, thus cutting off Thanet. While one division held the line, the other was to march east to their main objective, Manston Aerodrome. Also, vital for their supply lines was the capture of Margate, Broadstairs and Ramsgate harbours. Another objective was to be the Motive Power Department at Ramsgate, where up to 30 locomotives were housed, alongside numerous goods wagons with all their loading facilities. Adjacent were the carriage sidings, should it be necessary to move the troops by rail. Once Thanet had been occupied as a base, the enemy could then spearhead towards Dover and London.

Local preparations

To combat this menace, all the seven slipways in Birchington were blocked with steel and concrete, amidst miles and miles of barbed wire. The slipway at Beresford Gap had 35ft sheer banks either side. When the concrete wall levelled with this, it resembled a dam. All this work was done with great speed. Owen and I were fascinated with the dumper trucks carrying the mixed concrete to the gaps. With the pull of a lever, they would shoot their load down into the wooden shuttering. We watched for hours – "If only *we* could do that!" we said.

Without telling anyone, we found some wood from a neighbour's fence, knocked down by the troops during training and built our shuttering 2 ft square. We then dug earth from the back garden and mixed it with water. Using our sister's doll's pram, which made a lovely dumper, we filled it to the brim with mud. Having made three good pillars, we were very pleased with ourselves. When mother saw what we had done she wailed, "Wait till your father sees this!" Then my sister showed her the pram, which we had hidden. When father came home and saw our 'handiwork', he exclaimed, "I'm not touching that garden again until they all grow up!" We were punished by not being allowed out to play. We also had to destroy our wonderful pillars, which were 3-4 ft high. We had to spread the earth evenly back over the garden again. Lastly, we had to wash the doll's pram, inside and out, with a hose and scrubbing brushes. Father actually did do the garden again, because we needed the vegetables!

Invasion Imminent

Workmen came along to cut down the iron railings and all the names of streets and railway stations were removed. My father remarked, "With all the Germans who've been living here, they would know their way around anyway." A deep shaft was sunk in the road beside Minnis Bay Tea Pavilion. Owen and I watched and wondered how they could get a naval gun down there from a vertical to a horizontal position. We learned later it was to be used to flood the sea with oil.

A large detached cottage called 'Gay Cottage', stood at the end of our road on high ground opposite Minnis Bay Hotel. It had a commanding position with uninterrupted views across the Bay to Reculver. From the outside appearance it looked normal, but inside it was turned into a fortress, with 3-4 ft concrete going down underground, as my father was later to be shown.

Eight coaches stood on the downside siding at Birchington railway station, ready to take the remaining residents away within an hour, if necessary. Each household would be allowed only one suitcase. Mother said it would hold only vital essentials – there would be no room for any toys.

Fall of France

A few days later my father read out from the newspaper that France had fallen. My mother told everyone we met and looked more worried than ever. My father read Winston Churchill's speech from the newspaper – "The events which have happened in France in the last fortnight have not come to me with any sense of surprise. Indeed, I indicated a fortnight ago as clearly as I could to the House that the worst possibilities were open and I made it perfectly clear that whatever happened in France would make no difference to the resolve of Britain and the British Empire to fight on – if necessary for years – if necessary alone. "What General Weygand called the 'Battle of France' is over. I expect that the 'Battle of Britain' is about to begin. Upon this battle depends the survival of the Christian civilisation ...... and if the British Commonwealth and Empire lasts for a thousand years, men will still say, 'This was their finest hour'. "

"Is this it?"

Although we did not have many toys, those we had were cherished. The thought of anyone taking over our house, which meant everything to us, filled us with hatred towards Germany. Should it happen without warning, we kept a long-handled axe behind the dining room door, determined we would get at least one of them. My parents had been told by the troops that if we saw yellow lights on the horizon at sea, that was the signal that the invasion had started. One evening, early in June, my parents were having a quiet drink in the Minnis Bay Hotel when they noticed all the troops were wearing plimsoles. Suddenly the bar emptied. As my parents came out of the bar and stood at the top of the steps looking out to sea, there they saw yellow lights all along the horizon.

They ran home as fast as they could and rushed indoors, followed almost immediately by a policeman's knock. He came to tell us to be ready in the hall with a suitcase when he came back to take us to the station. We stood waiting in silence; in my pocket was my favourite toy, a small clockwork tinplate bird with one leg missing. Time stood still – "It looks like this is it!" said my father quietly. Still we waited for what seemed like an eternity. Then came the dreaded knock at the door – the policeman came to tell us to 'stand down'! Later that evening, from our back doorstep, we looked left towards Pegwell and Sandwich Bays, where an orange glow lit up the pitch darkness of the blackout. My parents

heard in the following weeks that a 'German invasion' had been attempted along Sandwich Flats – and then oil on the sea was set alight. My father also heard there were dead Germans caught on the barbed wire and lying along the shore for weeks. No one could get to them, as the area was heavily mined.

The air raids had begun by now and Owen recorded the warning sirens in an exercise book. (See overleaf) The large 5.25 anti-aircraft guns were installed at Cleve Court and Dent-de-Lion. The shell bursts from these were black and much higher than the 3.7 smaller guns that had white shell bursts. The police called at our house to ask if we had any firearms. We had an air rifle so they took out the inner mechanism from the barrel and returned it to us as they left. We discovered that we could still fire corks from it, though.

Our parents gave us a serious talking-to about the dangers we were going to come across. My mother, with her sister Maud, had worked in the munitions factory at Woolwich Arsenal during W.W. 1, dealing with lidite, cordite and other volatile explosives. We were warned of the grave dangers of picking up anything unusual. They taught us which were safe and what not to do. Mother's words left an impression on us all. "You seldom get a second chance."

Spies

One dark evening, my father was riding his bicycle slowly home along Grenham Road beside the boundary hedge of Grenham House, a private school for boys, when there was a challenge of "Halt – who goes there?" Unable to see anyone, he concluded it was someone fooling about, so carried on riding. A shot rang out – he had never dismounted so fast! A soldier stepped out from the bushes with a rifle in his hands, telling my father he was lucky to be alive and asking why he didn't stop when challenged. After examining my father's identity card and finding out he was with the police at RAF Manston, his attitude changed, explaining they could not take any chances as they suspected that there were spies in the area.

My parents had already become suspicious of two old ladies, who always went out arm in arm together, faces always covered with a veil, collars turned up and hats pulled down, although it was summertime. They did not come from Minnis Bay, as we knew everyone before the war started, and the odd one or two who had come since. If only we could get a good look at them! Then my mother came up with

Air. Raides.

Tuesday, December 10th, 1940. 2.
Wednesday, December 11th, 1940. 7.
Thursday, December 12th, 1940. 6.
Friday, December 13th, 1940. 3.
Saturday, December 14th, 1940. 2.
Sunday, December 15th, 1940. 4.
Monday, December 16th, 1940. 4.
Tuesday, December 17th, 1940. 7.
Wednesday, December 18th, 1940. 1.
Thursday, December 19th, 1940. 4.
Friday, December 20th, 1940. 7.
Saturday, December 21st, 1940. 3.
Sunday, December 22nd, 1940. 2.
Monday, December 23rd, 1940. 8.
Tuesday, December 24th, 1940. 1.
Wednesday, December 25th, 1940. 1.
Thursday, December 26th, 1940. 1.
Friday, December 27th, 1940. 2.
Saturday, December 28th, 1940. 1.

Air Raides

Sunday, December 29th, 1940. 3.
Monday, December 30th, 1940. 3.
Tuesday, December 31st, 1940. 4.
Wednesday, January 1st, 1941. 4.
Thursday, January 2nd, 1941. 7.
Friday, January 3rd, 1941. 3.
Saturday, January 4th, 1941. 6.
Sunday, January 5th, 1941. 8.
Monday, January 6th, 1941. 6.
Tuesday, January 7th, 1941. 5.
Wednesday, January 8th, 1941. -.
Thursday, January 9th, 1941. 10.
Friday, January 10th, 1941. 4.
Saturday, January 11th, 1941. 4.
Sunday, January 12th, 1941. 4.
Monday, January 13th, 1941. 3.
Tuesday, January 14th, 1941. -.
Wednesday, January 15th, 1941. 4.
Thursday, January 16th, 1941. 7.

From my brother Owen's notebook. His mis-spelling of the word "Raides" was due to lack of schooling during the war.

a bright idea. She put my sister and me in the pushchair with a blanket over us so that only our faces were showing. I was told to lie back so that I could get a good look upwards at them under the brims of their hats. The two old ladies were walking slowly towards us on the pavement in Ethelbert Road – they always walked very slowly.

I was able to look up and get a fairly good view, certainly better than anyone else could have done. They both looked down menacingly as we passed. When we got home, my parents wanted

Some of our cigarette cards used by Derek and me to help us identify the aircraft

to know what they looked like. I said their faces were 'grey', as were their features! As children, we were inquisitive to know what Germans looked like, as we had been told that they had 'grey' faces! On numerous occasions, we witnessed the troops checking the ladies' identity cards and other papers, so they must have been in order. My father said he thought the two 'walked like men'. That evening he determined to find out where they went, so he got on his bicycle and spotted them walking slowly up the hill in Arthur Road towards Harold Road. It was dusk, so he followed them from quite distance, when suddenly they looked back, saw my father and ran! Yes, ran '"like the wind", with father in hot pursuit. They appeared to veer left into Harold Road. He was not far behind them, but when he reached the corner, they were no longer in sight. He searched the roads, including the service roads in the immediate vicinity to Ethelbert Road, in case they had doubled back, but found no sign of them. He came home disconsolate – they had just disappeared – never to be seen again!

Battle of Britain
We, in Birchington, were in the front line of the battle that was about to begin. The enemy bombers with our own fighter planes after them, often turned tail, dropped their bombs anywhere and beat a hasty retreat back to France. The danger was that these stray bombs could land anywhere and any time, often

before the air raid warning was sounded. With Birchington being only a village with very few shops still open, there were times we had to catch the bus to Margate. On one such occasion, from the top deck we saw the remains of a bungalow that had had a direct hit from a stray bomb opposite Domneva Road at Westgate.

The enemy planes had a menacing, pulsating drone designed to drive fear into us and break our morale. First of all we would see specks in the sky, with the sound getting louder. Then we recognized them – Dornier Do17Zs, Heinkel He111s and Junkers Ju88s. These bombers were escorted by Messerschmitt BF 110C fighter-bombers and Messerschmitt BF 109E fighters – wave after wave of them. Owen and I had aircraft recognition books and cigarette cards, so we knew them all, including our own.

Sometimes the raids seemed to be continuous – as one all-clear siren sounded, so the next warning followed immediately afterwards. Hanging out of our bedroom windows at the back of the house, we could see our Spitfires, Hurricanes and sometimes a Boulton-Paul Defiant, as they left the end of the runway at Manston, often climbing right in front of us. We had a grandstand view as they went to intercept the enemy formations. Not long after we had watched the 'dog fights', the vapour trails could be seen criss-crossing the blue, cloudless sky. This went on day after day, week after week, for three months. After each raid, we saw our fighters returning to Manston to re-fuel and re-arm, before taking flight again as another raid approached. The South East corner of England became known as 'Hellfire Corner'.

While the 'Battle of Britain' raged high in the skies above, work had to be done. Because my mother had elected to stay behind with us children, she had to do work for the war effort. As there were no factories in the area, she was put to work on the land – refusal would have meant imprisonment. We walked the half-mile to Upper

Dangerous Coastline

Gore End Farm in Minnis Road. Then we piled into the back of the trailer with mother, alongside all the other women, the only man being Mr Pemble, the tractor driver. From here he took us through all the road-blocks manned by troops, identity cards having to be shown every time, then along the Thanet Way, where we zig-zagged between the huge 'H' girders embedded in the road and grass verges. From here, we turned off into the fields towards the railway line, where we helped mother picking up potatoes, or whatever else needed to be done. We were miles from hearing the nearest air raid siren, so this was where the knowledge of all the aircraft that Owen and I had acquired proved invaluable. When an enemy aircraft approached, especially the fighters and bombers, which often came in very low over the sea, we would shout a warning and everyone threw themselves flat on the ground, except Mr Pemble. He always hid under his tractor. Sometimes, when we were strafed with machine gun fire, Owen would remark to me afterwards that if the tractor had been hit, Mr Pemble would have gone up with the explosion!

One day Owen and I were standing on our Anderson Shelter and mother was standing by its entrance right behind us, as we watched a Messerschmitt BF 109E, the top Nazi fighter, flying very low, almost overhead, but over the sea. Suddenly it climbed, turned and dived towards us. My mother grabbed an ankle each of Owen and I, pulling us off balance. We rolled down the side of the shelter and looking up we saw the flashes from its machine guns. Shell cases were falling in the garden and on either side of us. One bullet went through our rear fence into the lane. It looked as if it must have passed right where Owen and I had been standing seconds before. Later, we went and found the bullet and cartridge in the lane and showed it to mother. "That bullet was meant for you two", she said. My father replied, "It's true what they said in the last war – the only good German is a dead one." He was livid!

We had a block of four-storey houses backing onto us, but at the rear of the next row of houses towards the sea. In our own road was an area between Egbert and Arthur Road that had been excavated to about ten feet deep, with sloping sides. It had become overgrown with grass, small shrubs and trees here and there, and contained discarded prams, pushchairs and an old bicycle. It was an ideal playing area, which we named 'our dip' (as against the official 'Dip' nearer the sea in Minnis

Road). Our parents, should they want us, had only to walk from our back gate 10 yards along the lane and across Egbert Road to call us. (See Map 3 on p.38)

An enemy plane had flown in from over the sea, heading towards Sandwich, when from our back garden, we saw someone bale out. The parachutist came down in Arthur Road, in front of the 'art-deco' house called 'The Nore'. He was in a white flying suit with a brown flying helmet. He released himself from his parachute, which he left lying in the road. Looking back, he took out his pistol and ran up Arthur Road towards Harold Road. My father quickly got on his bicycle and tailed him from a safe distance, my mother calling after him, "Be careful – he's got a gun!" But again, after searching all the likely places, which he knew like the back of his hand, there was no trace – he had just disappeared – as the two strange 'ladies' had done!

By now the London Irish Regiment was billeted near us, adding to the build-up of troops in the area. We watched them from our back doorstep, training in full battle order, rifles with fixed bayonets, running and jumping over all the back garden fences. One of them slipped in our garden, badly cutting his hand as he fell on his bayonet. A lot of the fences were knocked down as a result of these manoeuvres, including the one between the end house and ours. We could walk across their garden to the retaining boundary wall with a drop of 7 feet into Egbert Road. One evening, a hushed voice in a Lancashire accent called from the direction of Egbert Road, "Got a cake!" We rushed over to the wall, where a large fruit cake was handed up to us. This was the beginning of many such gifts. We kept the back door open, listening for the whispered tones of a north country accent. The back door was never locked at night or when we went out.

When the air raids were overhead, only then did we run the gauntlet of shrapnel, as it slid down the roof tiles into the garden. Owen claimed a large piece that had fallen in Egbert Road. He bent down to pick it up, but dropped it immediately. It was still hot and burnt his fingers! He retrieved it later, when it had cooled down. In the courtyard of the Minnis Bay Hotel facing the sea, a searchlight had been installed, so Owen wanted to see it in action. He did not have long to wait before an enemy night bomber was caught in the beam, but before our A.A. guns had time to fire, the Luftwaffe pilot dived down the beam. Shouts of "Extinguish!" came, with everyone scattering and diving for cover. There was

"The Nore", an art-deco house in Arthur Road, where we saw the German parachutist land

a burst of machine gun fire from the aircraft, with bullets flying everywhere, but luckily there were no casualties.

We had a privet hedge bordering onto the rear lane, beneath which we discovered an incendiary bomb that had failed to ignite. Owen and I thought it looked like a 2" mortar bomb and wanted to keep it, but my father tried to keep us away from it until the A. R. P. could come and take it away. We were annoyed and went into the lane with our sister and started throwing stones. Seeing this, mother came down to us and wrenched the stone out of Owen's hand. "I told you not to throw stones!" she said. "You'll break a window." With that, she threw Owen's stone as far as she could – straight through next-door's kitchen window!

Mother took us to see the searchlight in the daytime. We had not been there long when a Heinkel He 111 flew in so low that we could see the pilot as it passed overhead. Mother asked a soldier on a mounted machine gun why he did not fire at it. "I have to get the order to fire first." was the reply. The aircraft carried on without a single shot being fired at it. We went home feeling very angry. Here was a German bomber they could not have missed. We suspected something was not as it should be – something was very wrong.

There was an Open day at the Royal School for the Deaf at Victoria Road, Margate, to raise funds for the war effort, so our mother took us there by bus. Among the crowd was a group of airmen from

Manston, whose faces were badly burnt. It brought home to us the horrors of war and we felt how brave they were to mingle with us – a real inspiration to us all. In the grounds was an undamaged Messerschmitt B.F.109E with camouflage netting over it. To raise extra money, there was a charge of 6d to sit in the cockpit, which we all did in turn. Owen, who was always mechanically minded, fiddled with the instruments and wiring while sitting in the pilot's seat. Suddenly, to our amazement, he started the propeller turning, which caught in the camouflage netting. Panic stations! An airman quickly jumped up onto the wing, diving his hand under the control panel and stopped the engine, kindly telling Owen he would make a good pilot when he was old enough! The church opposite the Deaf School had caught the blast from a bomb some while before and had then been shored up with huge baulks of timber, stretching halfway across the road.

Uncle Ernie

Uncle Ernie was a born pianist, who, during the silent film days, played at the back of a cinema screen owned by another uncle. Many an argument went on by cinema-goers saying, "No one could play like that – it must be a Pianola." He played by ear, so when the disbelievers were taken back stage to meet him, they had to humbly apologise. He had offers to play in high places, even a trial for the B.B.C. Radio. He turned them all down for his quiet life, although he would sometimes play on the piano in the pub that he frequented. When he and his wife Maud and daughter Gloria came to stay with us, he would play on our piano for hours. Passers-by would stop to listen to his magic touch. Our milkman, Charlie, would stop his delivery and was invited in to listen spellbound. He would have stayed longer, but my father gently reminded him that his customers were waiting for him! Charlie, who lived in Crescent Road, Birchington, was called up, so was now in army uniform. Our mother took us to pay him a visit to see his uniform, but we were more interested in his .303 rifle, which he let us handle.

The rationing of food was brought home to us when mother showed us exactly what we were allowed each week. We did not see a banana, an orange or any other fruit from abroad. As the majority of the population of Minnis Bay had left with the imminent threat of invasion, we were free to roam and go scrumping in the back gardens of many of the empty houses. However, we had to watch out for our Special Reserve Constable, who lived not far from us in Grenham Bay Avenue. We felt that the owners would not be back for a long time and it seemed a pity to see all that lovely fruit going to waste as autumn set in! At meal times we children would save the best piece of our small meat ration to eat until last. We discussed at length whether we should eat it first, in case the house got a direct hit with a bomb. We reasoned that if we waited, we might never get to eat that last choice piece ....!

Local shops

The owner of a baker's in Birchington was, we heard, a whiskey drinker and enjoyed her tipple. One day, while we were in the bread queue with our mother, a little inoffensive old lady was standing in front of us. The owner – you could smell the whiskey on her breath – was swaying from side to side. Looking at the old lady with bleary eyes, she asked, "What are you looking at?" The poor woman was lost for words and just muttered, "I'm not looking at anything." The owner fixed her with a withering look and replied, "For looking at me like that, you'll get no bread!" After we had been served, we left the shop and went round the corner, to find the old lady crying. Mother, along with other customers who had just been served, each gave her some of their ration, to make sure she did not go hungry.

Further along the road was a tobacconist and sweet shop, the owner of which was also a 'tyrant'. He was red-faced, with a scowl and would shout at us, "You can't have that – you haven't enough coupons!" Eventually, after buying what we could, he bellowed at us as we left the shop, "Shut the door!" It was the same every time we went to buy sweets.

A house in the village that had been bombed was in an unsafe condition, with just the outside wall left standing, with the rest of the building in rubble behind it. My father, who still had big arm muscles from his boxing days, was one of those selected to help pull it down. We all went to watch as the rope was threaded through a window frame and the men began to pull. We were very proud of him as it came crashing down, making a lot of dust as it hit the ground.

One day we watched a Dornier Do17 that had been hit and had smoke pouring from it, racing to see where it crashed. As it came down, we all cheered. The pilot, who had baled out over Brooks End, knocked at the door of a farmhouse and asked for a glass of whiskey. The farmer gave him one before he was arrested, but this caused feeling to run high in the village, as it was felt that the farmer must be pro-German and so was considered to be a traitor.

Early in September, there was the unmistakable drone of German bombers as wave after wave of them filled the sky. There must have been at least 1,000, all heading towards London. One appeared to be in the middle of a wave, surrounded by fighters. We children guessed that it was Goering and wondered if it was an airborne invasion, but thankfully it was not.

Grenham House School

We had recently noticed a lot of RAF Lorries with long cylinders on the back hidden under the trees in Darwin and Lyell Roads. One evening, as we were all going home from Birchington station via Lyell Road, we heard a high-pitched screeching sound. We were stopped by armed guards and told to go home via Minnis Road. The following evening, ever curious, we went back, but were stopped again, but in the meantime, the guards had heard who we were, so allowed us to venture forward. In the darkness of the courtyard of Grenham House School, which had been evacuated in 1940, we could just see a huge black or midnight blue balloon, attached to a wicker basket. The screeching came from the gas cylinders blowing up the balloons. When they were inflated, they took up the whole space of the courtyard. Then, gently swaying, each one was released, silently floating up and away towards France. We watched in silent amazement as one after the other took flight. The procedure only took place when the wind was in the right direction and the moon was right. We were told at the time that the baskets contained leaflets, but another source of information said it was guns with ammunition and explosives for the Resistance Movement in the occupied countries.

On another occasion, we watched as the Luftwaffe were being attacked by our Spitfires. One Messerschmitt was hit and the pilot baled out, so we all ran after him to see where he would land. We found him in Shakespeare Road, Birchington, dangling from a big tree under which stood half a dozen soldiers with fixed bayonets. Then the police turned up, followed by about twenty local people, to see the pilot taken prisoner and then led away. The aircraft, a Messerschmitt BF109E, had somehow missed all the houses and come down in a back garden on the north side of Crescent Road, Birchington. What we were after was the Perspex, but the police, who got there first, would not allow us near. We could see the plane all broken into small pieces, but we could not understand why this had happened. The pieces were usually quite large.

The Luftwaffe showed great interest in Plum Pudding Island, one mile to the west of the village, where the marshes began. They regularly targeted the area with H.E. bombs and enormous landmines, which they usually dropped at night with parachutes. There seemed to be something of great importance that Hitler wanted to destroy, but we were never allowed to venture anywhere near the area, with its armed guards – we also heard it was heavily mined.

One evening, just before bedtime, my sister and I were lying on the couch under the rear window, when suddenly the whole window was blown in onto us. The thick blackout curtain saved us from getting cut to pieces. At the same time, the explosion blew the back, front and hall doors off their hinges, the ceiling came down and all the gas-lights blew out. At first we thought we had received a direct hit from an H.E. bomb, but were soon to discover we had caught the blast from a land mine exploding between Plum Pudding Island and the rifle butts. The dust from the lathe and plaster ceilings was choking, but miraculously none of us was harmed.

At the end of the year we were still helping our mother out on the fields near Reculver, close to the railway line. Owen and I noticed an enemy fighter appear suddenly out of the clouds, bank and then dive. We shouted a warning and everyone threw themselves flat onto the ground, as there was no cover anywhere near. A passenger train from Victoria to Ramsgate was racing across the marshes, hauled by a Schools Class No 931 'Kings Wimbledon' at 90mph. It wasn't us the Luftwaffe pilot was after, but the train. There was a burst of machine gun fire as the train carried on towards Birchington. One of the crew on the footplate had been hit and was taken to Margate Hospital, where he later died. As most of the locomotives on this line were No 931 'Kings Wimbledon', they were later fitted with armoured cabs.

Farm workers from Brooksend Farm from W.W.2. Mr Eastland is third from right.

'The Spirit of Britain'
An example of morale boosting postcards issued
during the war

Chapter 4

1941

Manston

As all the schools were still closed down, our parents were doing their best to educate us, but sometimes our lessons were interrupted by 'tip-and-run' raids. The destination of most heavy raids was London and we were on the flight path, with the worst time being at night. We used to feel safe in the pitch darkness, until one night the bombers kept circling round and round. We guessed they were looking for Manston, where they eventually released their bombs. We heard the bombs whistling down, followed by the explosions. The searchlights were trying to pick them up and the A.A. guns were trying to knock them out of the sky. This became a nightly performance. One night they dropped what we called a chandelier. It stayed airborne as if fixed by a static balloon, as the brightness lit everything up like daylight – it was frightening. The heavy A.A. guns fired salvo after salvo, knocking pieces from it, until eventually it was extinguished – then we felt safe again.

While these raids were taking place, the German woman who lived almost opposite to us returned, after being away for a while. We heard the A.R.P. Warden calling out "Put that light out!" It was always an upstairs window with the curtains drawn back, making a glowing beacon of light in the night. Why she was never interned, was a mystery.

One of father's drawings,
which we thought was very good.

Home amusements

In the evenings when there were no raids, we played cards, taking turns to play crib with our parents, but the favourite game was darts, which did not go without its mishaps. On one occasion Owen threw a dart, which bounced off the wire between the numbers on the dartboard and flew into our sister's head. On another evening Owen (again!) missed the dartboard completely and the dart made a hole right through a willow pattern plate on the Welsh dresser, adjacent to the board. Sometimes of an evening we did drawing. My father would draw characters. Then out would come the huge dictionary, which we kept opening at random, testing our father with his spelling. There was not a word that he could not spell. We children often used to discuss what we would do if we were taken by surprise and a German paratrooper came into the house. We decided that we would bite his fingers off, but then we had second thoughts, because we thought the germs on his fingers would poison us – wasn't that why they were called 'Germ-ans'?

The food situation was getting desperate. Mother said that if we did not eat the food that was put in front of us, there was nothing else – we would have to go hungry. Needless to say, we ate everything – there was no waste in our house.

Land Mine

We stood in the lookout post over the promenade toilets opposite Minnis Bay Hotel one day, watching a huge land mine coming into shore. It had spikes and a soldier, with a .303 Lee Enfield rifle, tried unsuccessfully to hit one of the bobbing spikes as it gradually made its way towards the promenade on the high tide. Although we were behind sandbags, one of the half dozen troops standing round said, "If it goes up, so will half Minnis Bay!" The Naval Bomb Disposal Unit from Chatham had been alerted when it was first spotted. We noticed it was significantly bigger than any of the other mines we had seen – and this observation was with only a small proportion of the mine showing above the waves. We all held our breath, as it washed ever nearer towards the slipway. It was now only a matter of yards away from striking the promenade or slipway with one of its spikes.

As soon as the Bomb Disposal Unit arrived, two sailors immediately jumped fully clothed into the sea in front of the mine – by now it was just three feet away from the promenade. Using themselves as a human buffer, they clung onto the spikes, the mine ever turning, so that they constantly had to change position. At one stage their backs were against the promenade and the mine was squashing them. They held on like this until the tide turned and then receded, leaving the mine stationary on the soft sand. From the lookout post, we watched them carefully disarm it and when they had completed the task, they drove up to us. "It's harmless now," one of them said, showing us the gleaming detonator. I thought it looked like a 25-pounder shell case. The mine was an enormous, black one, with German writing in white. Two of the sailors sat on top of it as they drove it away – how brave they had been. To combat this menace, an R.A.F. Vickers Wellington, with a huge degaussing (or demagnetising) ring nearly the size of the aircraft hanging beneath it, flew low over the sea. We called the Wellington 'the ringer'. As we watched, the submerged mines popped up to the surface, where they were fired on and exploded.

Germ warfare?

One day, after an enemy aircraft had flown over we found strips of dull silver paper, two feet long by one inch wide, everywhere. Word got round that it had been dropped to foil our radar system, but shortly after handling it, I began to itch, which quickly intensified. The only relief was to scratch the spot until it bled. It affected my arms, legs, chest, neck and throat. One could see what my mother called a 'parasite' moving around under the skin. Not only did the whole family catch it from me, but everyone with whom we came in contact, it spread so quickly. Everyone became covered in scratch marks and blood and we could not concentrate on anything, because the itching was so relentless and contagious. We were alarmed and word got round that the silver paper was impregnated. Could this be the start of germ warfare by Nazi Germany?

When father came home from his job, he too was affected. I will not repeat what he said, except to say that the air was blue! The Local Health Officer, Nurse Davies, visited our house with strict instructions for mother to have ready a sulphur bath as hot as we could stand, then she would visit us at the appointed time.

Each one in turn had to immerse themselves in the sulphur – what a smell! Then we had to stand up and while still wet, the nurse, used what looked like a decorator's brush, and painted us all over with a substance resembling wallpaper paste. As she did so, the irritation stopped immediately. The paste covered the infected area and the relief was wonderful. My mother asked what the paste-like solution was, but the nurse simply said, "Here is a small bottle; if the itching re-occurs, apply the contents with a small brush." To our great relief, we never had to use the mysterious bottle with the strange, pungent smelling contents.

Smuggling

We had a call at the back door from the Customs and Excise Officer. He was accompanied by the Special War Reserve Policeman, who was well known to us. He lived in the next road and was hated by all and sundry, including the troops. Mother, along with us three children, had witnessed him stopping two soldiers on a bicycle in Grenham Road. One soldier was giving a lift to the other on his crossbar and the 'Special' took out his notebook and booked him! The Customs Officer asked if we knew anything (which we didn't) about some lard that had been washed up on the beach. They then proceeded to search the house. While this was going on, I was looking out of the window down our back garden, where my father had grown lots of runner beans. The poles ran the length of the garden right next to the garden path. It resembled a hedge, but what attracted my attention was that there were flocks of birds on the runner beans.

After the search, the 'Special' made a report in his notebook, constantly asking the Customs Officer how to spell the simplest words. The look on the Customs Officer's face said it all. After they had gone, I told my parents about the birds on the bean row, so they went to investigate. There, hidden amongst the beans, was a wooden crate with "Pure North American Lard" stamped on the side. Where the sea had got at it, the lard was discoloured, but when this was scraped away, the inside was perfect. The local rag-and-bone man had hidden it, so that he would not get caught. He had a tradesman's cycle, with a large carrier on the front, ideal for the purpose. Word got around among the troops – they seemed to know everything that was going on! We sampled the lard in our mother's cooking and there was nothing wrong with it. Soon, more lard was washed in onto the beach – to be hidden among the beans once more. My mother conferred with the troops, saying, "If you could supply the ingredients, flour, sugar, dried fruit, meat etc., I will do the cooking for you." Oh, how they appreciated it – home cooking, instead of the usual cookhouse food.

They gave us more cap-badges, shoulder flashes and anything else they could lay their hands on. When we were out of earshot of our parents, they asked if we had any older sisters and looked very disappointed when we told them we hadn't. The Customs Officer never called again – my father reckoned he knew what was going on and turned a blind eye.

The Blitz

From an early age, I had suffered from an allergy, so I was taken up to Great Ormond Street Hospital in London to find the cause. We all went, except my father, who was working. We had to get up very early, as the train (the 'workman's') left Birchington station at 5.00 am for London. At Gillingham, where the electric trains began, we had to get off and go up some stairs for another ticket. While mother went to get the new tickets, a porter on the platform said we should

This sight was repeated all over the City and the surrounding area, during London's Blitz

25

get back on the train. Fortunately, we stayed on the platform waiting for mother to return, because the train pulled out before mother could get back with the new tickets. So we simply caught the next train.

Prior to our visit, our father had written to two maiden aunts – his sisters – who lived in Islington, to say we would be visiting London and why. Lettie and Clara were very kind ladies who met us at Victoria Station. When we arrived, they said there had already been an air raid that morning. As we went out of the front of the station, my sister saw some pigeons in the road. Thinking they would get run over, she dashed into the road to rescue them, but was very nearly run over by a double decker bus herself! In the hospital, I had different pieces of tape stuck on my arm which turned different colours, to try and find out what I was allergic to.

When we came out of the hospital, there were dozens of fire engines with their hoses crossed over each other, like spaghetti, fighting a fire next to the hospital. We went back to Islington with my aunts and had tea – strawberries and jelly. What a luxury! Later on we had to leave for home, but it was already dark by the time we got to Victoria Station. My mother and sister got into the carriage next to the engine, while Owen and I went to see what was to haul us. On the notice boards of all the stations was a notice saying "Is your journey really necessary?" Here we were in the London Blitz, with another air raid about to start. We wanted to get out of London as quickly as possible. We knew that if Stewarts Lane Locomotive sheds had been hit, we could have a 0-6-0 C class goods engine, or something similar, resulting in a very slow journey home.

To our delight, at the front of our train stood No 917 'Ardingly', R.E. Maunsell's famous 'Schools' class, the most powerful and fastest 4-4-0 in Europe. Half of the class were modified with a Lemaitre multiple jet blast-pipe and larger diameter chimney, which made them free steaming and faster still. This modification also applied to the No 921 'Shrewsbury'. Owen and I each had our favourite engines, his being the No 918 'Hurstpierpoint', but here stood mine, the No 917, painted in unlined black with side windows blanked off and steel plates to hide the glow from the firebox at night. Also the tarpaulin sheeting from the back edge of the cab roof to the front of the tender was already in place. This was also to stop the glare, which could easily be seen by an enemy aircraft at night. During the daytime, this tarpaulin was rolled underneath the cab roof.

The air raid siren was already going again as the train pulled out up the steep incline over Grosvenor Bridge across the Thames. Owen and I looked out of the windows in the corridor, making sure that no lights were showing.

To our horror, No 917 slipped, then gained her feet, then slipped again. Huge pieces of red-hot coal were showered skywards. We looked up at searchlights everywhere; they had caught a Heinkel He111 in their beam, but worse – it was overhead, as we crossed the Thames. The A.A. guns were firing flat out, the bombs whistling down and exploding. Once over the river, the line flattens out; then the No 917 started to pick up speed, faster and ever faster. What a relief – we had a clear road with no red signals. The further we got out of the suburbs and into the countryside, the safer we felt. As we stopped at Newington near Sittingbourne my sister, aged 5, lifted the blind to see where we were, and seeing the name inside the booking hall, exclaimed "Ooh – Newcastle!" A man opposite, who had been asleep all this time, leapt up shouting "No!" and looked out. As soon as *he* saw the name, he slipped back into his seat with the knowledge that he had not travelled 300 miles north, instead of 41 miles east! Our interest in trains was life-long.

Exercises

The 'dip' just behind our house, our favourite playing area, was taken over by the army at this period, for training exercises with Lloyd Carriers (very similar to Bren-gun carriers), using the banks on either side to good effect. One alarming feature of these tanks was the amount of broken tracks when they were trying to climb the steep gradients. Owen and I discussed this and agreed it could be the fault of unskilled drivers, or, if it was fault of the vehicles and was not rectified, could make us lose the war. We eventually saw the lessons had been learnt, when more exercises were undertaken in 1944 in the same area.

Laundry van

All the vehicles on the roads were either military, public service or tradesmen. Owen and I were watching another air raid out of our open bedroom window as usual, when we noticed a civilian laundry van travelling along Arthur Road (a side road) at high speed. We could see it was not going to stop at the main Minnis Road, but, travelling along this towards the sea, was a small army Tilley van. There was a high hedge surrounding the property on the corner, obscuring it from view to the side road, and so the two collided. From our vantage point, the laundry van was at fault, colliding with the Tilley. Luckily, no one was hurt, but we did look on the laundry van as the 'enemy' from then on.

Tanks

The deep sound of tanks rumbling took us running to the corner of Minnis and Dane Road, where, to our amazement, a convoy of Churchill tanks was coming down Minnis Road at full speed. They turned left into

Some of the badges given to Owen and me by the soldiers billeted at Minnis Bay, Birchington

Dane Road at 90° without slowing down. The inside track was locked, in order to bring the tank round. The result was that after they had all gone through, the road at the corner of that junction was a pile of churned up chalk. They proceeded towards Plum Pudding Island, near the rifle butts. We judged this as later we heard them firing from this direction. We would have liked to watch them, but we were never allowed to that area. Armed guards patrolled the entrance to it and we also heard that it was heavily mined.

Later in the day, the tanks returned, churning up the same corner again, but now right across the road. When they had all gone, the local council man had to mend the road on his own, and all by hand – with no mechanical devices to help him. No wonder Owen and I did not think he looked too happy! The next day it would be the same – and so it went on, day after day, but we were never able to find out where the

tanks came from. We heard that there were tanks hidden under the trees at Dent-de-Lion in Garlinge, so we always went on the upper deck of the bus to and from Margate, where you could look down amongst the trees, but we saw no sign of them.

U Boat
Another day, I was walking by myself past the Minnis Bay Hotel, when I noticed the tide was high. As I wandered along the Parade on the grass near the cliff edge between Harold Road and Hereward Avenue, to my amazement, I saw a German U Boat surface in broad daylight approximately a quarter of a mile from the cliff edge. Within seconds, a shot was fired at it from the coastal naval guns near the Winter Gardens, Margate, I think. The U Boat had nearly submerged when another shot was fired at it, but neither shot hit its target.

Dangerous Coastline

Fifth Columnist

Streete Court at Westgate, lying on the bus route to Margate and recently taken over by the R.A.F., had received a direct hit from enemy bombers, causing many casualties. We saw the ruins from the top deck of the bus and mother said "There's a Fifth Columnist in our midst. Every time our boys are billeted in a large building, it receives a direct hit." She was so angry – then I think she cried a little.

25-Pounders

An army officer called one morning to ask if we would open all our windows. Mother enquired the reason for this. "We are going to fire 25-pounders at the back of your house and if the windows are shut, the explosion could shatter them." We asked if we could watch and he agreed, so with great delight, we went to Charles Field beside Canute Road. Under the trees lining the field were three 25-pounders. Up until then, I had the impression the shell and case were fixed together, like a .303 bullet. It was only when the gunners were putting the coloured bags into the shell cases that I realised the difference. We were allowed to stand quite near and we thought these were quite loud – till they began using the armour piercing shells! Mother asked afterwards where the shells had landed and we were told "off North Foreland".
(See Map 3 on p.38)

New Friends

R.A.F. Manston was now being strengthened with more personnel drafted in. Two families, whose fathers worked at Manston aerodrome, moved in to Minnis Bay. The first to move into the next row of houses to ours in Ethelbert Road was Brian, a little older than me. He had a younger brother Peter aged two. We quickly struck up a friendship, as also did our parents. Their house was more modern than ours – they had electricity! I was impressed watching Brian's mother using a vacuum cleaner. Shortly afterwards, Peter and his family moved into a detached bungalow in Dane Road, behind the last row of shops in Minnis Road. He had a sister aged three, called Valerie, who became a playmate for our sister and his parents joined Brian's and my parents in social get-togethers. Brian had moved form Hornsey in North London, while Peter came from Fulham, S.W. London and was a supporter of Chelsea Football Club, the same one that Owen and I supported.

My father and Owen were walking our dog, a smooth-haired fox terrier, and returning along a footpath from Church House to Kent Gardens, Birchington. To the left were open views across to Reculver Towers, where, from that direction they saw a bomber approaching very low. Father commented, "It's O.K. – it's one of ours." Owen blurted out, "It's

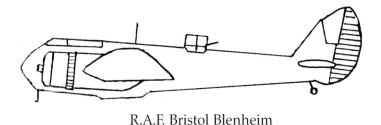

R.A.F. Bristol Blenheim

The two planes had many similarities, especially when the Ju 88 had R.A.F. markings

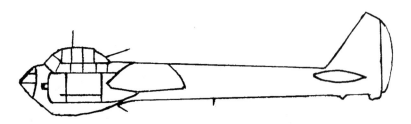

Luftwaffe Junkers Ju 88

Drawings by Derek Hart

not! It's a Ju 88 with R.A.F. markings!" It was so low and so near, they could see the aircrew with the gunner sitting behind his machine gun. Father said, "He could have just swung his gun round on us!" It flew on towards Margate and then they heard the sound of bombs exploding. We later heard that one of the bombs fell on No 5 platform at Margate Railway station.

We were very restricted with having no transport and, living where we did, we were more or less isolated. Since mother always carried the identity cards, we had to go with her. Father had his bicycle, which only he could ride, so we had to make our own amusement. Our sister used to dress our two pet rabbits, named Spick and Span in dolls' clothes, then sat them up at each end of her doll's pram, with an eiderdown between them. Neither of them struggled to get away, in fact they did not seem to mind at all, as she wheeled them round the back garden talking to them all the time. They looked like 'Tales from Beatrix Potter'! Owen and I played with the few Dinky cars we had, but sometimes, in the evening between the air raids, which went on day and night at this period, my father would box, with open hands against Owen and me together. He was so quick that, even with two to one, we could rarely touch him. Mother taught us to say our prayers with her from an early age and now always ended with a special one for all the soldiers, sailors and airmen.

With the German invasion of Russia in the summer of 1941, father studied the newspapers daily, conferring with mother, while we children listened intently. As the Germans penetrated deeper into Soviet territory, father predicted, "This is Hitler's biggest mistake. The Russians are leading them into a trap. When the Russian winter sets in, the German army will never get out alive. They will not be able to advance or retreat. They don't have the equipment or clothing to survive. They will be frozen alive – not like the Russians, who are properly equipped for this terrain." In the following months, everything he had foreseen happened. It was wonderful to listen to my father, an educated man, who had given great thought to all the theatres of war. He gave us courage and uplifted our spirits to carry on.

Lord Haw Haw

Among the extra troops who moved in to Minnis Bay was an R.A.F. officer with his wife and baby. They occupied the house called 'The Nore', where, the previous year, the Luftwaffe parachutist had landed in the road. My mother would occasionally baby-sit for them. William Joyce, the traitor known as 'Lord Haw Haw', must have been well informed, because his broadcast that evening quoted "a film currently showing at the Regal Cinema in Margate is entitled 'Target for Tonight' – that will be our target for tonight." This propaganda was treated with contempt by the civilian and Armed Forces alike. My mother baby-sat while the officer and his wife went to see the film at the Regal. They got back home safely, but later that night, there was an air raid and the cinema got a direct hit, along with its twin, the Astoria in Northdown Road, but they were both empty.

The top of the toilet block at Minnis Bay was used as a look-out post during the war.
It was from here that we watched the huge mine being made safe.

Six of these aircraft took off from Manston to fight the might of the German Fleet, as it broke out of Brest

The memorial to the Fleet Air Arm at Manston Spitfire Museum.

Chapter 5

1942

School

The schools reopened during this year, but only on a part-time basis and with many interruptions. When the air raid warning sounded we had to go down into the long shelter, where the teachers carried on the lesson. The trouble was, if you were at the far end of the shelter you could not hear what they were trying to teach, so we had an elderly lady teacher who got us to sing songs like "Mares eat oats and does eat oats", which I thought was a waste of time. Going home, we were let out in ones and twos, because, if we left en masse, there was a chance that we might have been machine-gunned by the odd enemy fighter plane coming out of the clouds. Even so, on more than one occasion, we were fired upon. Later on, if there was a shell warning for more than two hours, we were sent home.

German warships

On February 12th, we realised there was something going on out at sea, as most of the troops were making their way down to the sea front, so we followed. There, on the horizon away to the east, were three large German warships. We were informed they were the Scharnhorst, Gneisenau and Prinz Eugen. They sailed along the horizon in broad daylight. This was German arrogance at its worst, believing they were the "ruler of the seas" and that we would not dare to interrupt the safe passage of their prized "pride of the fleet". On everybody's lips was the question "Why don't we do something?" Sadly, in the following day's newspaper, my father read out that six of our Fairy Swordfish planes, armed with torpedoes, took off from Manston to engage the ships, never to return.

[The episode became known as "The Channel Dash" and is now commemorated in Manston Museum. The Birchington Heritage Trust has recently been given a copy of the story of this momentous event, by the author and one time resident in Birchington, Edward Powell.]

Beach

Part of the beach and promenade was now open, so to supplement the meagre coal ration we went 'wooding' – collecting the driftwood washed up along the shore. We were paid by the Customs for any large pieces over 6 ft long, also for any rubber, essential for our war effort. All along the shore we found hundreds of round floaters approximately 6 inches in diameter and 2 inches thick, filled with air. We filled countless sandbags with them and took them to the Customs men. To convey the wood and rubber from the beach we used the pram, which was well sprung and could take 2 cwt a trip. We three children had been collecting wood, some of it over 6 ft long, when we spotted a mine coming in on the tide. We were on our way home and could see 'our' Special Constable waiting for us by the Tea Pavilion. Owen quickly put his initials on the underside of the large pieces of wood in chalk. The Special told us to leave the wood and go home, as there was a mine coming in. Later we went to retrieve the wood, but it had gone, so we told mother. Knowing where he lived, we looked in his front garden and sure enough, there was our wood with Owen's initials on it! Mother reported this to the Customs, who paid her for the wood – they knew what he was like.

Owen and I had a secret hoard of .303 live rounds dropped in the trenches, as well as spent smoke screen 2" mortar bombs, .303 cartridge cases and an assortment of live and spent ones from Sten Guns and Revolvers, plus others we were not quite sure of. This was hidden in the basement toilet outside the house opposite our back garden. We showed it all to Brian and Peter, but instilled into them what was safe and what was dangerous. We told them on no account to touch mortars – there were dozens, some of them coloured grey. These were smoke screen bombs and did not explode, so when we found them, they were intact but an empty shell. The high explosive type was coloured brown with red and green rings at the opposite end to the fin. Sometimes, when we found one of these, it had been fired but had failed to explode, so we knew that it was highly dangerous and informed the troops where it was. A twelve year old boy was killed by one of these mortars at Reculver during 1942.

A small selection of the huge collection of ammunition we amassed during the war.

Stick of bombs

One bad night, Owen, Brian, Peter and I were in our back bedroom, with both windows wide open, hanging out of the windows to get a better view of the low flying Luftwaffe bombers. They were flying in circles right overhead, so we knew they were after something important. Our searchlight picked them out and the A.A. opened up 3.7 and 5.25s – shrapnel cascaded down the roofs all around us. Amidst all this we suddenly heard a 'clang-clang', to which Brian remarked, "The trains are shunting late in the goods yard at Birchington Station tonight." Owen, quick as a flash, shouted, "That's not trains shunting, that's the bombs hitting the bomb doors as they drop!" He was right! As we all dived under the beds, we heard them whistling down. We counted to 15, all holding our breath – but no explosions – just silence, except for the bombers flying away.

Next day, as we walked up Minnis Road with mother, we found out that the bombs had all fallen on open agricultural land near Gordon Square and behind Upper Gore End Farm, then out towards Plum Pudding Island. We had had a lot of rain recently so the ground was very soft. A house in Gordon Square that bordered onto the farmland had a narrow miss, as one of the bombs had dropped into the field, within feet of it. The mud from the impact reached right to the top wall of the house. We learnt from the troops at the scene that the Poles, who were being forced to help make the bombs, had sabotaged all those dropped the night before. As far as we knew, the bombs were never dug up.

Truant

One day, my sister and I were walking to school with Brian. We were already late leaving and Mr Troke, the headmaster, had reprimanded us for being late before. My excuse then was I had to get the coal in. We hurried along, but feared we were in big trouble. When we were halfway there, Brian suggested that we played truant, and only return home at the usual home time. He assured us that our parents would not know. I had the notion that he had done this before in London. So we wandered back down Minnis Road and under the railway bridge. Then we followed the path on the right, round the edge of the agricultural field adjacent to Grenham House Lodge, a bungalow on the corner of Grenham Road and opposite Green Road, but by now, in the school grounds. Not being fenced off, we wandered through the trees for camouflage, until we got to the bungalow, where we found a sash window wide open at the bottom. Looking in, we saw an array of weapons, some of which we had never seen before. After checking there were no guards or troops to be seen, we climbed in the window. We went through all the rooms, each one stacked to capacity with rifles, all sorts of machine guns, and anti-tank devices.

We went back to the first room we had seen, where I made sure there were no live rounds up the breeches. Then we played 'soldiers' for three hours, mainly with .303 Lea-Enfield rifles and machine guns, making sure no one touched live ammunition. We had a wonderful time, and later, as we felt hungry, we ate our sandwiches, which we had brought for our school lunches. None of us had a watch, but I kept an eye on the trains going by, as I knew what class of engine was allocated to the train timetable. (The railway line was clearly visible from the bungalow in 1942.) I knew that sometimes substitutions were made, also additional trains were laid on and there could be disruptions because of the war. Taking all this into account, we eventually climbed out of the window and made our way home.

Brian's mother was very fastidious in keeping him clean and tidy. Our mother gave us a quick look, sensing something was wrong. What we did not realise was how dusty we had got traipsing through the fields and woods, and the oil from the weapons on our hands and clothes also gave the game away. Brian's mother got the truth out of him and marched him along to our house. Then there was 'hell to pay'! Our punishment was not being allowed out to play for a week – to us, this was worse than anything! Later that evening we heard our parents talking. "If children could spend

Band of the 7ᵗʰ Battalion The Hampshire Regiment in the Square at Birchington c. 1942
There appears to be a form of tank-trap positioned each side of the road,
beside the white markings.

three hours in Grenham Lodge without being seen, what if others we have seen ("spies?" we thought) found out? It is hard to contemplate." The very same thing had crossed my mind on the way home.

Parachutes

There were now Hawker Typhoons stationed at Manston. We found this very encouraging, because they carried rockets for attacking enemy tanks, marshalling yards, etc. with devastating effect. Around this time, we were finding a lot of small, white silk parachutes all over the place, with nothing attached to them. Some of the children took them to school, tied a stone or piece of wood to the end and threw them up into the air, where they floated gracefully down. The strings, also made of silk, would sometimes start to plait from the base, gradually working upwards to the parachute, eventually making it inoperable. We were told that they carried a flare, but could never substantiate this.

Mortar bomb

Owen and I were walking along the cliff top at Grenham Bay, when we came across a mortar bomb in the long grass. It was not the usual 2" flat-ended type, but the larger 3" one, shaped like a small aerial bomb, mid-green in colour, with a deep 4" orange band from the front end. We had a sandbag with us for collecting dandelions and grass for our rabbits. (We also had a pet hen called Sheila, but she did not need anything special to eat as she ate more or less what we had, besides pecking the grit from the road near our back garden. The eggs she laid sometimes had double yokes, which helped supplement the food rationing.) Owen placed the mortar in the sandbag, but unknown to us, a police constable, not our local one, had seen this, and came over to ask what was in the sandbag. Owen replied, "Food for our rabbits." "And anything else?" enquired the P.C. "Yes, a trench Mortar." Owen replied. We gently tipped out the contents onto the grass. "Hmm, you'd better let me have that", and so the P.C. took it away. We were a little disappointed at the time, but came to the conclusion it was all for the best. It was an 'unknown' to us.

Canterbury

The almost nightly drone of German bombers overhead, on their way to London, was always worse than in the daytime. One particular night, it was heavier than ever. Mother commented, "Some poor devils are going to get it tonight." We soon found out it was not far away. We were in contact with the troops all the time, so they soon informed us that Canterbury was the target that night. We followed the troops to the top of Brooks End Hill, on the outskirts of Birchington. There in the night sky, eleven miles S.W. was an orange glow – Canterbury was on fire! In the next day's newspapers, it was reported that 2,142 incendiary bombs were dropped on the old city that night.

Sea Shore

Another time, I was walking along the cliff top with mother, when I looked out at the incoming tide, which had nearly reached the cliffs by then. There on the shoreline was a stretch that was all red. Asking what it was, there were a few moments' silence, before mother, who was very upset, replied, "It's probably one of our airmen who has been shot down over the sea."

Storm

During an electric storm – the air raids continued, no matter how bad the weather was – I spotted a Focker Wolfe 189B, a twin fuselage aircraft, very similar to the P38 Lockheed Lightning of the U.S. Air Force. It had just passed over towards Manston, when it was struck by fork lightning. Smoke immediately started to stream from it, then a member of the crew baled out, with the aircraft losing height, until it went out of sight behind the tall houses opposite.

Homestead Farm

Mother, along with the other ladies, was transferred from Marshside Farm near Reculver, to Homestead Farm, which borders Park Road, Birchington and has views across the fields to Broadstairs. She had to start at 7.30am, so we helped her on the fields for an hour, then walked the quarter of a mile across the grass to school. After school, we returned to help her until she finished. One morning, not long after we arrived, two German fighter-bombers

St George's Street, Canterbury, soon after the Blitz of 1st June 1942

attacked the gas works at the end of Linksfield Road at Westgate, just half a mile away. We saw the bombs dropping! It looked as if they could not possibly miss the gasometer – we expected to see a massive explosion any second, but we only heard the bombs exploding – the gas works were intact as the raiders fled towards the sea. We heard later that one of the bombs came down at an angle, aquaplaned on the water and oil mix surrounding the base of the gasometer, then careered upwards, taking a chimney pot off the farmhouse opposite. It then carried on to explode harmlessly in the farmer's field beyond. *(See Map 4 p. 49)*

The Westgate gasometer and gasworks can be seen at the top of the picture, across the fields of Homestead Farm

Chapter 6

1943

Westfield Road bomb

Our mother took us to the shops in Birchington in mid-January. We walked the mile journey, as no buses ran to Minnis Bay. Late on the previous night there had been an air raid and we saw bombs dropping in the centre of the village, followed by explosions. When we reached the shops, we learnt that a terraced house, No: 66 Westfield Road, had received a direct hit. The houses on either side, though damaged, were still standing. We went to see if we could help. The local fire brigade were there as well as the A.R.P., but the two old ladies who lived there lost their lives. Mother knew them both, so she was very upset.

Lancasters & the Bouncing Bombs

An Avro Lancaster, which was approaching very low towards the front of our house, sent us all dashing out of the back door, for a better view. Not much above the rooftops, it passed directly over our house with its bomb doors wide open. In the bomb bay, we could clearly see what looked like a barrel, spinning slowly. The flight took it low over the sea till just before Reculver Towers, when it dropped its barrel. This bounced along the surface of the sea; once it had stopped bouncing, it sank, but without an explosion. Then came another doing exactly the same, then another. It became quite a spectacle – a daily routine – with us all hanging out of our rear bedroom windows to get a better view. When, in mid-May, we read in the newspapers of the success of our bombers bursting the Mohne and Eder dams, we still did not know until some time later that we had witnessed the vital practice runs for this achievement.

Air raid

I needed a new coat, so mother made arrangements with Brian's mother, so that we could all take the bus to Margate. We would all walk to Birchington Station and get on the Margate Harbour bus that arrived at 12.55, just before the shop, White Fuller's, closed for lunch at 1.00pm. It was just two or three shops up from the bottom of the High Street. It was June and a lovely day and Brian had been playing with us, getting himself into a rather grubby state! His mother took one look at him, and after giving him a smack, said

she couldn't take him out in that state, and would have to clean him up.

This resulted in delaying us, so we knew we would miss the 12.40 bus from Birchington Station. While having lunch, another air raid took place, then we took the next bus into Margate. As we alighted at the Harbour, we could see that the bottom of the High Street was cordoned off. When we looked up the High Street, we saw White Fuller's had received a direct hit. All that remained was a heap of rubble. My mother asked the A.R.P. warden standing guard, "What time did it happen?" "Just after one o'clock." His words were ringing in our ears as we just stood there in silence, thinking "If we had caught the earlier bus ...."

Cinema

Normally we went to the Ritz Cinema in Birchington, but Owen wanted to see "The Cat and the Canary", showing at the Carlton Cinema at Westgate. Mother took us three children to Birchington Station, then by bus to Westgate. As we were about to go into the cinema, Owen noticed R.A.F. lorries hidden under the trees on the corner of Westgate Bay Avenue and St Mildred's Road. The film, starring Bob Hope and Paulette Goddard, was about three-quarters through when the air raid siren sounded. As it was situated on the roof of the cinema, when it went off, the noise was deafening, being only 30-40 feet above us. The film was immediately stopped and everyone made a hasty exit. By now it was pitch dark outside, with no streetlights. Because of this we took a wrong turn, but managed to retrace our steps, and run back to the bus stop at the corner of Minster Road and Canterbury Road. This raid turned out to be a really heavy local one, and not one on its way to London, as it normally was. The searchlights picked out the planes, with the ack-ack guns going full blast, salvo after salvo. The enemy bombers were going round and round in circles and must have been after Manston or some other local target.

Eventually the bus came slowly along, a small blue light just visible at the front. At the terminus at Birchington station, mother told my sister and me to get into the pushchair. She then took off her shoes and with Owen beside us ran down Minnis Road. The raid was at its height with shrapnel raining down. We could hear it hitting the roofs of the houses on our right. To our left, the bombs were dropping onto the open farmland, probably mistaken for Manston. We finally fell into our air raid shelter in a big heap, thankful to get safely home – it was a nightmare journey!

Bottle of yellow 'lemonade'

Soon after, Owen, Brian, Peter and I were walking along the beach, as the tide was out, until we reached Beresford Gap, with its chalk pools – there was no sand in this area. Simultaneously Brian and Peter spotted a bottle shaped like a hip-flask with a crimped metal cap, which looked like a bottle of lemonade. They both picked it up together, each claiming it was their find and they were going to drink it. It then developed into a tug-of-war with the bottle. "It's mine! I saw it first!" exclaimed Brian. "No, it's mine!" claimed Peter. Owen, being five years older than us and therefore much taller, snatched it away from both of them. Holding it high above our heads, with Brian and Peter still trying to retrieve it, Owen exclaimed, "It looks a bit cloudy to me – neither of you will have it." Then he threw it, 'mills bomb' fashion, onto the chalky rocks off the beach. There was a massive flash as the bottle broke, then it started to emit smoke, increasing every second, with the westerly breeze taking

it towards Westgate. We realised it was a smoke screen bomb, and ran back along the beach towards Grenham Bay, where the troops had a rope for scaling the cliffs from the beach. Once on the top, we gained a vantage spot towards the Beresford Gap.

The whole of the beach from that spot eastwards was obliterated with dense black smoke. We realised it must have been seen and expected a knock at the door after we arrived home. We expected the local P.C., the A.R.P. or the army to arrive at any moment, but none came. So, later on, we went back to the cliff top at Grenham Bay to see if anything had happened. The flames had died down, but it was still smoking, although diluted in intensity. To our surprise, there was no one about. It was eerie, so we quickly made our way home.

High Explosive Mortar

After the exercises by the troops, we went along the trenches that they had dug. We would find dozens of live rounds of .303 bullets as well as the spent .303 cases. We took all these back to our 'camp' basement toilets in the large Victorian houses that backed onto our house. We put all these, plus spent mortars (smoke screens) into tin baths, until they were brimming over. We then built more 'camps' at the trench ends, making a false end on them and covering the top. Into these we put the light bulbs we had found on the beach. While we were on the beach, Brian said he knew where there was a mortar, so Peter and I asked if it was grey. Brian assured us it was. He came running back holding it by its fin and stood in front of us. To our horror, we saw it was brown with red and green rings – the high explosive type. He proudly held it up to reveal the end cap had come off, showing the explosive charge inside.

Calmly Peter and I (Owen was not with us this time) told him to lay it gently onto the sand – then we ran. Brian queried our instructions, but Peter and I stayed calm and from some distance, we were most insistent that he obeyed our instructions. A look of fear came over Brian's face – for a second, we thought he was going to throw it over his shoulder and run – but he did as we told him, then all three of us ran as fast as we could away from it. The incoming tide covered it, so the next day we went to the same spot, but it had gone. We told Brian what we thought of him in no uncertain terms and that we were all lucky to still be alive!

The Ritz Cinema in Station Road Birchington

Bullets

By now, a lot of the children at school who had found live .303 rounds, talked of opening them up, pouring the gunpowder into a dish and lighting it. Owen went into our shed, took the bullet out of a .303, poured out the gunpowder, then hit the percussion cap with a hammer and nail. The noise was deafening – he never did it again! Some of the rounds contained thin strands of cordite. These we pushed into the brick walls then lit the end. It was not enclosed so it did not explode, but just flared up.

Hand grenade

We had a newcomer to Minnis Bay whose father was also in the R.A.F. at Manston. Ronnie was younger than we were, and a bit silly. We warned him of the dangers, but he persisted in following us, although we did not want him. One day, he turned up with a 'friend', a man we knew was a bit odd, and Ronnie declared that he knew where there was a Mill's bomb. We knew there were none in the area and thought that Ronnie was just trying to act big. Being younger than us, he wanted to 'make his mark'. "All right – I'll show you where it is" he announced. (See Map 3 overleaf)

Brian, Peter and I were on the lower, pink promenade, near to where it terminated by the Minnis Bay Hotel. Ronnie and his friend were on top of the black promenade, which was four feet higher and extends backwards to a rough decorated brick wall/ shelter. From a cavity in the wall, Ronnie took out a loose brick, from behind which he took out a Mill's bomb. To our horror, he laughed as he took out the pin then threw it at us. It bounced on the pink promenade, went between us and then rolled. We three were transfixed to the spot in disbelief – we seemed to be frozen – time stood still for what seemed like an eternity!

Suddenly we broke from our stupor, ran away as fast as we could, then threw ourselves to the ground. We waited for the explosion and prayed that the blast would go over the top of us. We waited, heads on the ground – there was silence. Eventually we raised our heads to find the grenade, still intact, had rolled to the edge of the promenade 15 yards away. Ronnie's friend had already gone. We then dealt with Ronnie, 'good and proper', never to see him again. The tide was in, with the grenade one foot from the water's edge. We wondered what should be done about it till eventually Peter volunteered to deal with it. He took a long run and kicked it into the sea!

Barrage balloon

We had no barrage balloons in our area, so to see one float 20 – 30 feet from the ground was quite a sight. It was being carried above the lower end of Minnis Road towards the railway bridge, with its steel hawser

Minnis Bay seafront beside the Minnis Bay Hotel.
The two levels of the promenade can be clearly seen in the top corner of the photo.

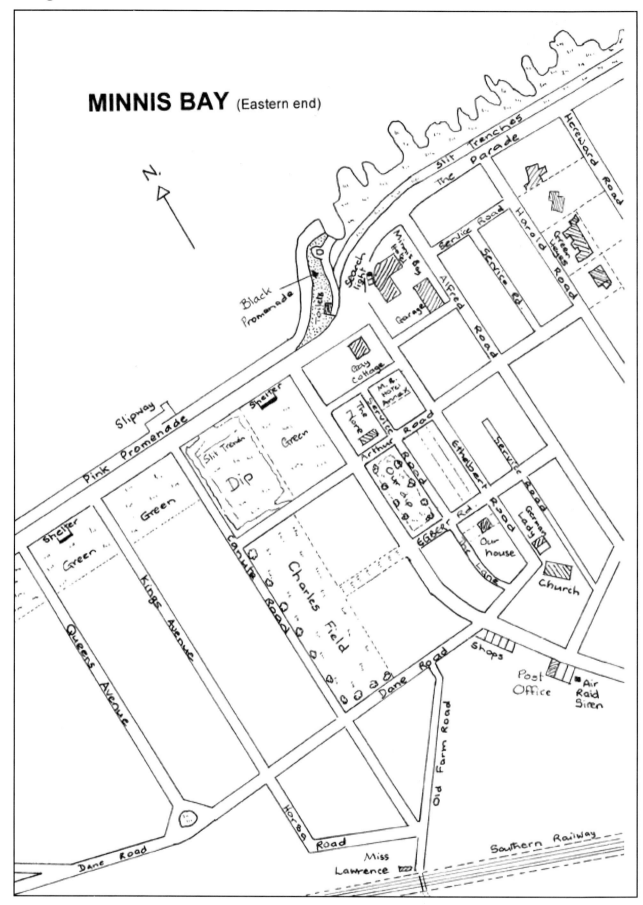

MAP 3
Enlargement of the eastern end of Minnis Bay, Birichington.

dangling beneath it. When it got to the corner of St Mildred's Avenue, it began to rise, but the wire became entangled in the chimney pots on the corner house. Instead of this bringing the balloon to a halt, it careered on, bring down part of the chimneystack. I followed it as far as the railway, where it gathered more height. I never did find out where it ended up!

Molotov Cocktails

Brian, Peter and I were at the trenches, as usual, when we found ourselves at the end of one by Beresford Gap. A concrete wall had been built across the gap to the height of the cliff top – the wall resembled a dam. We noticed a small hole at the trench end, so we dug away with our hands, until we revealed a secret, hidden room, overlooking the whole gap and the wall. Inside the 'room' were dozens of Molotov Cocktails. We had seen these on the news at the cinemas, but knew very little about them. There was no one about, so we threw a few over the top, where they smashed at the foot of the 'dam'. Nothing happened – but unknown to us was that they either had to be primed or else the fuse lit, before being thrown.

A huge mine

One day, I was by myself as I wandered along the beach towards Beresford Gap, and rounded a corner, looking as usual into the caves. I walked towards one that started from an inlet of about 25 yards. I had nearly reached the entrance, when my attention was diverted to a small cave to my left. There, lodged out of sight from the beach, was an enormous mine, similar, but without spikes, to the one the Bomb Disposal Squad from Chatham had made safe two years ago. I was small for my age – my father said I ought to be a jockey – just four feet tall. I looked up at this huge, round object, six feet high and shiny black with German writing stencilled on it. I was just a few feet from it and the sight of it took me by surprise – it was frightening. I turned tail and ran along the beach, all the way back home, where I told my mother, who immediately informed the authorities.

P. I .A.T. bombs
(Personnel Infantry Anti-Tank)

Along the stretch of the cliffs from the Minnis Bay Hotel to Grenham Bay, were dozens upon dozens of P.I.A.T. bomb fins protruding, 25 ft high from the beach. The bombs themselves were buried into the chalk. We knew these were for practice; otherwise there would not have been much of the cliff face left – or of the fins – if they had exploded.

We knew what they were, as we had seen them at an open exhibition at the British Home Stores in Margate High Street. (Only the upper High Street level of the store was being used at this time. The lower, sea front level was blocked off and the stairs down to this were blocked off with wooden floorboards. I do not remember going down to the lower section.) In the entrance to the store was an empty sea mine with a slot cut in the top, into which the public dropped their money, as there was no entrance fee. Mother put in what she could afford, as it was all in aid of the War Effort. Inside the store, we saw P.I.A.T. bombs, as well as 'sticky' bombs, also for anti-tank use. These two were the only bombs we had not seen before. The rest were quite common to us by now, although we had seen some strange looking grenade launchers and machine guns.

Gas

There was a shortage of petrol, so measures were introduced to use alternative fuels for essential services. Some of the double decker buses, called 'Guy Arabs', which had wooden slatted seats, towed a small trailer with an engine mounted on it to produce gas propulsion. We would always sit just inside the rear platform of the bus, so that if the bus were to be strafed by the enemy, or be caught by an exploding bomb, as it sometimes was, we stood a good chance of jumping to safety. While sitting at the back, we could look out on the trailer, part of which got red-hot. The problem was, whenever we stopped at a bus stop or road junction, the choking smell

This mine, found on Deal beach in autumn 1943, is similar to those washed up at Minnis Bay

39

of gas would drift into the passenger area!

Another vehicle that used gas was the local laundry van. This was the one that Owen and I had viewed as hostile, after it crashed into the Tilley van in Minnis Bay in 1941. The laundry van was rather large and high, but on top of this was a huge gas-bag, covering the whole area of the roof.

Shops

We had to walk to Birchington village, as the few shops in Minnis Bay closed down at the outbreak of the war. The one-mile trek was often taken to stock up on food and other essentials. We often heard the whistling of bombs dropped by the Luftwaffe, quite frequently before the air raid siren warning. We would hold our breath and pray that it would miss us. On one occasion it was just 300yards away along Albion Road, which lies off Station Road. Morrison Bell House, a large building occupied by our troops, had received a direct hit. Mother asked if she could help, but was reassured by the A.R.P. that it was all being taken care of by the police, fire brigade and ambulance service. There must have been many casualties. (Fortunately none of them were fatal.) On the way home mother said, "It's always where our troops are billeted. We must have 5th Columnists in our midst." She was bitter and did not say any more, but I noticed tears in her eyes.

Toys

The Minnis Bay Hotel had its own huge garage at the rear of the premises in Alfred Road. It was used for servicing vehicles as well as having pumps for issuing petrol. The army had taken this over, partly for camouflaging their Bedford 3-tonners. We asked if we could have some of their empty tins of paint, to which they agreed. The tins still had a little paint in the bottom – green, brown and black – which was marvellous. We could not get any paint, and could not afford it anyway. With the paint we were able to transform some of our Dinky toys with authentic colours. Owen and I could not get any Dinky tanks, so we made our own out of trellis fencing slats. The angles seemed right for the tracks, then two blocks of wood, the larger one for the body and the smaller for the turret. Then a large nail with the head sawn off was banged into the turret, to become the gun. These were also given camouflage treatment and were greatly treasured. The paint was also used for our ships and aeroplanes.

A lot of swapping of toys went on between the four of us. Owen had a number of pre-war toys, as he was 5 years older than us. Peter would let me play with his large Dinky tank, but would never swap it. On the other hand, Brian swapped two W.W.I lorries, one with a revolving anti-aircraft gun mounted on the back. I painted it green and black. The other lorry had a revolving searchlight, which Owen painted brown and black.

Cooking

The new pink promenade, laid down just before the war started, only stretched from the Minnis Bay Hotel to the tea pavilion (now 'The Minnis'). Beyond this, towards Plum Pudding Island, were cliffs no higher than eight feet, where we could jump down onto soft sand any time, as the tide never came in this far. Our feet would sink in the sand up to our knees. Twice, while landing, my head came forward onto my bent knees, with the result of a black eye, much to the

Some of our toy soldiers from World War II

amusement of the others. I was walking along this stretch of the sand by myself, in the direction of Reculver, as I could smell a mixture of petrol and, to my surprise, something cooking. The smell got stronger as I approached a group of soldiers huddled round something. They saw me and beckoned me over to them. There was a mobile petrol stove – I had never seen such a thing before – and on the top of it was the largest slab of fruit-cake I had ever seen. It must have measured 2 foot square by 3 inches thick. I had arrived just in time to see it still intact and I was asked if I wanted a piece. I said I

Our toy vehicles from World War II

did! – then watched it being sliced up. The smell in the open air was wonderful – so was the cake! I thanked them and then made my way home. I thought at the time, they probably had to do this as an exercise in self-sufficiency – but what a nice exercise!

'Jane'
One summer day, Brian, Peter and I made our way to the east end of the pink promenade, on the lookout for anything interesting – bullets, shrapnel and such like. We came to the end where the cliffs had eroded, forming small coves, and the one in front of us being only ten feet wide. There sat an R.A.F. officer wearing just a pair of shorts, but with his uniform neatly folded up beside him. I had seen him in this uniform earlier. He was reading a book as he sat with his back to the cliffs. With him was a young lady, completely naked and prancing round in circles on the beach below, skipping over piles of seaweed. We stood silent, with our mouths dropped open and just stared! The couple did not see us as we silently backed away out of sight. We decided that the lady looked exactly like 'Jane' in the Daily Mirror, except that she had black hair, instead of blonde – then we continued looking for bullets!

Paravane
We had not seen a torpedo, so when Owen and I heard that 42 had been washed up at Beresford Gap, we were ready to go down and have a look, but our parents stopped us, saying it was too dangerous. A few days later, we were out walking with our mother at Coleman's Stairs Gap, when we saw what we thought at first was a torpedo, but it turned out to be a paravane. *(This was a torpedo-shaped device, towed from the bows of*

a vessel, so that the cables cut the anchors of any moored mines.)

Burning
The troops had not long finished an exercise in Charles Field and I was returning from the beach by myself. It was summertime and I was wearing a short-sleeved shirt. The bushes along the edge of Charles Field, including Arthur Road side, were covered in what looked like a deep brown sticky substance. I did not touch it, but as I walked away, I caught my bare arm on one of the branches and there was an immediate burning sensation. I ran home, and as there was no one at home, I washed my arm under the running cold water tap with Life Buoy soap. This did not ease the pain, so I just kept using the soap and water for at least half an hour until it finally eased. At the end of this time I was totally exhausted, but greatly relieved. I still had a slight burning feeling for a few more days. When I told my mother what had happened, she did not take kindly to it and just told me off for going near the bushes in the first place. I decided the troops must have been using phosphorous bombs.

Perspex
Whenever an aircraft crashed nearby, the main aim was to get to the wreckage first, because we wanted the Perspex. Invariably the Police or A.R.P. beat us to it, keeping us well away. More R.A.F. officers had moved into houses near us and our parents quickly got to know these new neighbours. They told them about our obsession with Perspex. "What do they want Perspex for?" asked a Flying Officer, while standing in our back garden. Owen replied, "To make a model

This Perspex plane is still a treasured family memento

aeroplane." He promised to make one for us. True to his word, in the following weeks, he presented us with a Perspex Hawker Typhoon, complete with R.A.F. roundels. He also gave us R.A.F. wings in brass.

Whirlwind

Our mother had taken the three of us up to Birchington to do the usual shopping. By now there were a few more shops open than at the outbreak of the war in 1939. We had got most of the shopping and were on our way back home. We had reached Station Approach, where Mr Bushell had a baker's shop, which always displayed lovely cakes. Mother was always tempted by these. We stood with mother and Mr Bushell in the middle of the road outside his shop. Mother was holding the cakes and talking to Mr Bushell, as there was no traffic except for the occasional bus or army vehicle.

Suddenly we heard the roar of low flying aircraft approaching from the direction of Birchington Square. A German bomber came into view, just above the rooftops. Right on its tail was a Westland Whirlwind, a twin-engined fighter-plane of the R.A.F., now at Manston. Its four cannons in the nose were blazing away. The bomber, a Dornier Do17, I believe, with black smoke pouring from its engines as it passed overhead, was disintegrating, with pieces of it falling onto the rooftops, amid empty shell cases.

The Whirlwind carried on firing – we could see the cannon shells ripping into the stricken bomber, the cartridge cases falling into the road. We cheered as we jumped up and down in the road. The two planes disappeared from sight over the railway bridge, while Owen and I collected some of the fallen debris. We heard later that the Dornier had crashed into the sea off Beresford Gap. "That's one less!" said Mr Bushell, as the Whirlwind made its way back to Manston.

A Military Band marching up Lyell Road, Birchington in c. 1943. The Bungalow Hotel can be seen behind them on the left, with the gables of Grenham House School in the background.

Chapter 7

1944

Songs

The word spread in the school playground about the bad treatment Germany was giving to our prisoners-of-war and the even worse atrocities carried out by the Japanese, not only to P.O.W.s but also to civilians. We felt defiant and sang songs with our own words, such as "Whistle while you work, Hitler is a twerp" – and so on! The most popular song was "Colonel Bogey", with all its daring swear words about Himmler and Goebbels, which we sang in the playground at the top of our voices. Afterwards, we felt quite brave that we had 'done our bit' to help win the war. Never once were we reprimanded by the teachers for using this bad language – yet they must have heard it!

"Chocolate"

A whisper went round the school that the Chemist's shop was selling chocolate without sweet coupons, so on our way home, my sister and I bought some – without coupons! We ate a bar each as we walked the mile home – but we only just made it in time – to the toilet! "No wonder you had to rush *there*," said mother. "You've been eating Exlax!"

Exercise

We learnt that General Alexander was now C-in-C Middle East. Back in 1941, there had been a big exercise on the green and in the Dip alongside Canute Road. Mother and we three children were allowed to watch. The troops also used the dip behind our house. Some of our troops pointed out to us that one of the observers that day was General Alexander, as well as other 'top brass'. The Lloyd Carriers were going up and down the steep banks, but without the broken tracks we had seen in 1941, much to the relief of Owen and me. They were mostly using smoke screen mortars and high explosives, which landed on the their target – a chalk outcrop on the beach. It was low tide and the outcrop was opposite Minnis Bay Tea Pavilion. All went well until a stray high explosive shell landed on the Tea Rooms, which were mainly glass beforehand – but not afterwards! We could even hear the glass shattering from where we stood, some distance away. A halt was called while a dispatch rider sped to the scene to make sure a fire had not broken out. Firing then resumed.

When it was all over and we were on our way back home, we felt more confident that we were going to win the war.

Football

The grass in Charles Field became very overgrown, but Brian, Peter and I decided to play football there. The central part of the field was trampled down where the troops were constantly using it for manoeuvres, making it suitable for our game. We were having a good time until Peter kicked the ball into the long, two-feet-high grass at the entrance to the field. Brian ran over to find the ball and we went over to help him. "I've got it!" he shouted – whereupon two heads bobbed up, one a hatless soldier, wearing a shirt, braces and no tunic, the other a young lady with dried grass in her hair. "Get out!" bellowed the irate soldier, so Brian grabbed the ball and ran – as we all did – and that finished our game of football!

Cheek!

Brian, Peter and I were playing on the upper edge of the Dip, adjacent to Minnis Road, when an attractive young woman, dressed in a two-piece suit and high heels, walked close by on our side of the footpath towards the sea. I believe I had seen her in the uniform of a WAAF officer – the one resembling "Jane" in the Daily Mirror, but with dark hair instead of blonde. Brian, who was more out-going than Peter and me, put two fingers in his mouth and gave a loud wolf-whistle. The young woman kept walking, ignoring him. Frustrated, he tried again, giving an even louder wolf-whistle, but she again turned a deaf ear. Unable to contain himself being ignored twice, he blew a loud 'raspberry' and called out after, "The old bag!", whereupon, she swung round on her heel, came up to Brian and then slapped him hard round the face.

Films

Our father was quite often away on War work, which took him to Didcot. He hated these trips and was always very relieved when his tour of duty finished. For a treat, mother would take us all, sometimes including Peter and Brian, to the Ritz Cinema in Birchington, when something good was showing. When it was finished, we only had the one-mile walk home, instead of the longer journey from

My interest in railways has never diminished, as this model railway shows.

The station in the model railway is an accurate copy of Birchington Station.

Westgate or Margate. Our favourites were Laurel and Hardy, then Abbot and Costello, especially when they starred in "Keep 'em Flying". Other films we enjoyed were "The Mark of Zorro", "The Four Feathers" and "They Died With Their Boots On". Of the war films, we enjoyed "The Foreman Went to France", "The Way Ahead", "The Flemish Flag", "One of Our Aircraft is Missing", "The Power And The Glory" with Conrad Veigt, and "Dangerous Moonlight".

The film that brought the war home to us all was "Went The Day Well?" when we realised what could happen to us at any time. We were always on the lookout for anything suspicious, but after seeing this film, we increased our vigilance one hundred percent. We informed mother, who told father about anything we had seen. He then reported it to the Liaison Officer at the Minnis Bay Hotel, whom they had known since 1940.

Scene from 'Went The Day Well?'

Railway

By 1944, Owen had left school. Owing to his fragmented education, caused by the constant air raids, shell warnings, the schools being closed for 18 months, and then resuming for mornings only, he had a struggle with his learning, especially mathematics. The headmaster, Mr Troke, wrote a high-handed letter to father on the subject. He was enraged and wrote back explaining the situation concerning his elder son. Still the headmaster was of the same opinion. An exchange of letters between them followed, resulting in my father setting the Headmaster a most difficult task in mathematics! The headmaster had to concede that it was beyond him, so Owen left to take on the job he had been doing on Saturday mornings,

while still at school. He was delivering fruit and vegetables on a trade bicycle for Fred Pettman, who had a shop in Station Road, Birchington. This shop was on the corner of Paddock Road and Station Road, where 'Blue Monday's' now stands. Soon afterwards, Owen attained his ambition of starting to work on the railway at the Motive Power Depot at Ramsgate Locomotive sheds, where he began as a locomotive cleaner. If he passed all his grades, he would then graduate to fireman and eventually to his goal of engine driver. This was also my ambition.

Owen had to cycle to work seven miles each way at all hours and in all weathers. He also had to get a permit from his workplace in order to buy a Starlight dynamo for his bike, as he was a priority worker. He always posed questions for me, mainly about the locomotives. 'See if you can notice anything unusual about 922 "Marlborough" – a Schools class locomotive'. A few days later, I saw "Marlborough", which had stopped on the down platform at Birchington. From my vantage point looking down from the railway bridge, I spotted the 'unusual' – it was a bullet-hole through the nameplate. It had been strafed by the Luftwaffe, similar to when we had seen the 931 "Kings-Wimbledon" shot-up along the marshes near Reculver, in December 1940.

Because of acute manpower shortage, the cleaners were called upon to do the job of fireman. Owen had already been firing on the footplate on various trips. One of these was on a munitions train going via Dover. His driver explained as the journey progressed, "We'll need a good head of steam when we get to Dover Priory, then if we get a clear road, we will have to go flat out after the right hand curve when we leave Archcliffe Tunnel, past Dover Marine Locomotive sheds, then the open stretch to Shakespeare Cliff Tunnel. The German long range guns will see us – you'll see the flashes from the other side (Calais), if you look to your left." Owen made sure the steam needle was right up, with the engine blowing off steam as they got to Dover Priory.

The signals were clear, with the train going like 'a bat out of hell'. Owen looked over towards France and sure enough, the flashes came, then the roar as the shells went overhead. One hit the chalk cliffs above them, bringing it down on the opposite track – this being only six feet away. Had it fallen on their track, the train, with hundreds of tons of ammunition would have been derailed, which almost certainly would have exploded. They carried on till they were in the safety of Shakespeare Cliff Tunnel.

During the war children in Kent's schools experienced many a lesson in shelters like this .

School

At school, we were still getting interruptions from shell warnings. Quite often, after two hours, we were walking homeward-bound across the playground, when the "all clear" siren was heard. The teachers came running out to call us back into our classrooms, but certain individuals made a dash for home. When questioned the next day as to why they had disobeyed an order, it was always the same excuse – they had not heard the teachers calling them to return!

6-Pounders

A new type of gun appeared on exercises on Charles Field. These were the 6-pounder anti-tank guns, similar to the 25-pounders, but with very small wheels, which the gunners rapidly detached, then re-fitted later. Unlike the 25-pounders, they had a long barrel and were very manoeuvrable, the troops handling them with ease. When they had finished the exercise, the towing vehicle was attached to the end of the barrel, from a coupling underneath. I was fascinated as they drove off with the guns facing the other way.

Jeep

A jeep had been parked in our back lane, just behind our house. As there was nobody in sight, I sat in the driver's seat, holding the steering wheel. I imagined I was driving it and started to see what all the knobs were for. I happened to push the self-starter, but did not know that it was still in gear. It leapt forward, but the engine did not fire. It was me that did the leaping, straight out of the driver's seat and right up our garden path and indoors!

Churchill

One day the news got around that Winston Churchill was to visit the area – we even knew the time he would pass through Birchington Square. We stood outside the Post Office to see him, as he approached from the direction of Minnis Bay. We waved to him as he sat in the back of a big black car. He returned our wave with his huge cigar in his hand and a broad smile on his face. We felt honoured to see the Leader of our Nation, who had brought us from the dark days of 1940, the miracle of Dunkirk and the threat of invasion, when we stood alone. We knew and felt this fear when we saw the invasion lights along the sea horizon, and realised that there was no one to help us. I had often thought that God must have sent this man, with his bulldog courage, to defy Hitler and treat him with contempt, when all seemed lost and we had little or no defence. As I made my way home, I kept wondering why he had visited this small dot on the map. Why not London, Dover, Portsmouth, Southampton, Plymouth, Bristol, Cardiff or Liverpool?*

What was there so vital and important that he had to see it for himself? My father often spoke of "Gay Cottage" at the end of our road. Civilians, whom we suspected were scientists, visited it at times. "A lot goes on underground there." I would often hear in his conversations with mother. If this were so, the enormous German mine was on target to destroy it, till the Naval Bomb Disposal Unit from Chatham defused it. I had seen many mines washing in and they were all roughly the same size, some with spikes. But the huge black one was perhaps for a special target, like the Barnes-Wallis bouncing bombs were to destroy the dams in the Ruhr.

There was also Plum Pudding Island, consisting of marshes and a sewage works. Why was it so heavily guarded by our troops, with civilians no allowed within three-quarters of a mile of the area? The Luftwaffe dropped numerous land mines by parachute in the vicinity. These were the most destructive – and the Germans were seldom wrong in their targets. There appeared to be something of vital importance and our parents had definite ideas of their own about the region.

See note at the end of this chapter

D-Day preparations

I saw one of the many posters on a board, which read, "Careless Talk Costs Lives". I thought how true this was, because if Germany had knowledge of Churchill's visit to Minnis Bay, by now a massive bombing raid would have taken place. Soon after his visit, all our aircraft seemed to be airborne, bearing black and white stripes under the wings and round the fuselage, some towing gliders. Owen and I particularly liked the Typhoons, with their rockets slung underneath the wings, for anti-tank 'busting'. The next day, when father read to us from the newspaper, we learnt that the Allies had landed in Normandy. We felt proud of all the soldiers who had been billeted around us and whom we had seen training over our back garden fences. After all those years of exercises, our family were fairly optimistic that we would win the war.

Secret weapon

One night, while we were all asleep on mattresses on the floor under the kitchen table as usual, we were woken by a harsh, low pitched roar, getting louder by the moment. We dashed to the back door and climbed up onto the coal box for a better view. Then, across the black sky in the direction of Manston, but on course for London, we could see a long red and yellow flame, not very high in the sky, but travelling faster than any fighter plane. Then followed the next one, then another and so on. In the newspapers the following day, we read that "Hitler's new

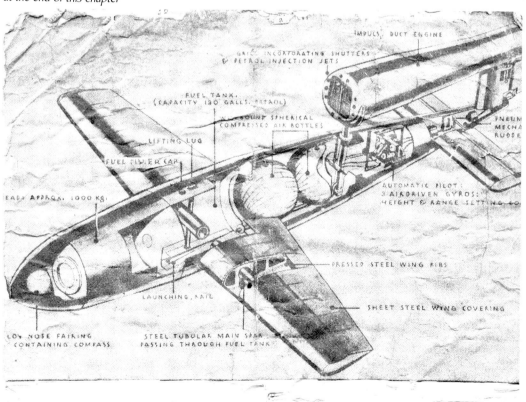

Father collected this picture from the newspaper

47

weapon" – the V.1. – had been launched on London. The next day we saw them in daylight – terrifying, pilotless, gyro-controlled, flying bombs. They had short wings and a rocket motor situated on top of the fuselage at the rear of one ton of high explosive. The Hawker Typhoon, and later the Hawker Tempest, did try to shoot them down, as did the ack-ack guns, which we saw bring down a number of them. The frightening situation was we did not have an aircraft that was capable of 500 mph. Later on, we heard that the Tempest's speed had been increased and their clipped wings had been strengthened. This was so that they could fly alongside to divert the V.1s by tipping their own wing tips against the rockets' wing tips and sending them off course – and this did succeed.

The terrible thing with what we now called "Doodlebugs" was the silence after the engine began to sputter and then stop completely. This was followed by the terrible SILENCE – a matter of only a few seconds. The short wings did not carry it far, so it would drop sharply and then there was an enormous explosion. This was always much more frightening at night. I would be asleep, but would wake immediately with the words, "Mum – Doodlebug!", but to start with I got the reply, "No it's not, go back to sleep." No one else heard anything for quite a while, then sure enough, the rest of the family heard it. At first they thought I was imagining it, then they came to realise that I was never wrong.

In undertones I heard my parents say, "He's right, you know", and we would all make our way out to the 'dugout' as we called our Anderson air raid shelter. From the entrance, we watched the flames from the jets propel them across the night sky, with the ack-ack trying to intercept them before they reached their target. At times they would be disrupted from their allotted course, but then arose the horrific danger that they could go anywhere, as we were soon to discover, until their fuel ran out. We held our breath in silence, then came the explosion and we breathed again ....

V. 1 off course

One day my sister and I had finished school for the day at Park Lane Primary School. We were not in a hurry as mother was working on the fields at Homestead Farm, behind Spurgeon's Homes. We had arranged to meet by the entrance to the Homes in Park Road, but as school finished at 4pm and the farm workers at 5pm, or just five or ten minutes before, we strolled the quarter of a mile across the open rough grassy field of the Memorial Recreation Ground, towards where mother was waiting

for us. She was standing at the roadside under a tree and we had almost reached her, when I heard a Doodlebug. Instinctively I looked to the right towards Quex Park, this being their usual flight path inland, but there was nothing to be seen. I swung round in the opposite direction and spotted it just clearing the school roof, coming straight towards us.

The rocket motor was already starting to sputter, as the V.1 lost height. Mother screamed, "Quick!" whereupon she grabbed us and pulled us down with her to the base of the tree. The rocket was coming straight at us – I said a silent prayer, "God, help us". We looked up as it hit the top of the tree just 20 feet above us. The roar from the enormous long flame at the back was ear splitting, and branches began showering down on us. As soon as it had passed over, the motor cut out. I thought it would nose-dive, then drop like a stone after hitting the top of the tree, into the field behind us. Somehow – just somehow – we watched as, with the motor now spent, it glided on for three-quarters of a mile, just missing "Ray House", the white, art-deco house in Sea Road Westgate, then over the cliff-top, where we lost sight of it. Seconds later came the explosion as it hit the sea.

We stood there watching where it had disappeared for a long time, nobody saying anything. It had all happened as if it was in slow motion, especially when it was directly overhead. I felt the heat from the jet blast as it passed. Mother and my sister both admitted that they too had said a prayer, when I told them that I had prayed. "The Lord has answered our prayers" mother replied. We were all still visibly shaken! (See Map 4 opposite)

V.2

The V.1s continued to come until Germany, with its clever scientists, produced an even more deadly and sophisticated weapon, the V.2 rocket, with no sight or sound of its approaching. There were rumours that one landed near Monkton, four miles away, but there was nothing to confirm this. One day, my mother and I were winkling on the beach west of Minnis Bay Tea Rooms. We had already filled some sandbags with winkles, which we would sell through the rag-and-bone man, transporting them in the old pram.

It was a perfect day, a blue, cloudless sky with very clear visibility. We stood up to stretch our backs – this was a backbreaking occupation. As we looked out over the sea, to our disbelief, we saw something resembling a very fine silver needle standing on its blunt end, at what looked like 12 feet above the far horizon to the east. It

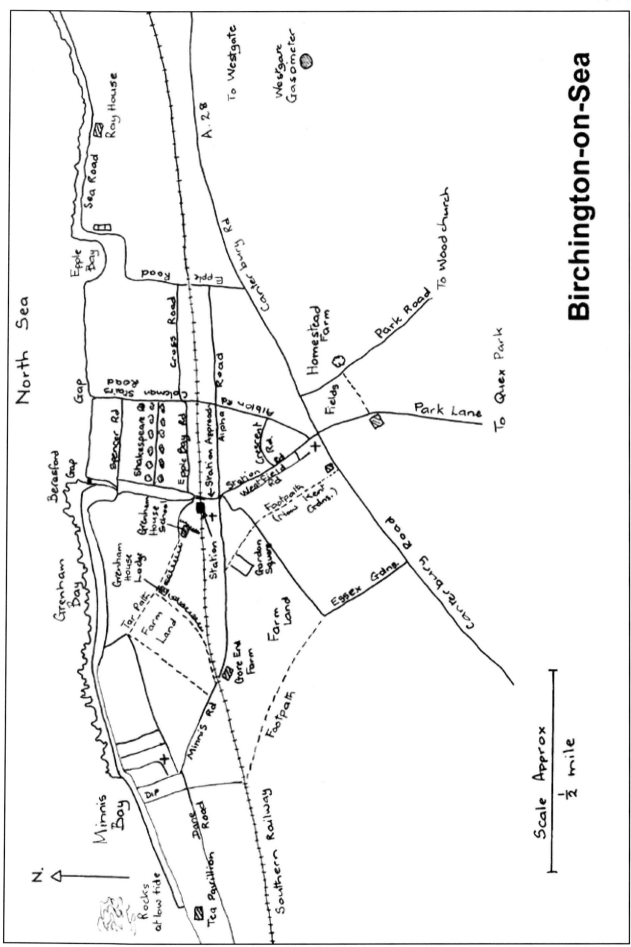

Birchington-on-Sea

MAP 4
Map showing the village and its outskirts.

Dangerous Coastline

was a V.2 rocket rising vertically, with a faint vapour trail following it. In the sun, it glistened silver, then the vapour stopped as we watched it climbing skywards until it disappeared. We puzzled as to where it was launched from. If mother had not confirmed that she too had seen it, I would have wondered whether my eyes were deceiving me. A distant explosion confirmed we were both right – sound carries well over water. "That has landed at Chatham", said my mother, looking terribly worried, then began to bite her nails, because my father was working at Chatham at that time. For the rest of that day and evening, we three children tried to console her that everything would be all right. Later that evening, when father eventually came home, she gave him a big hug and a kiss as he opened the front door. His first words were, "A V.2 landed at Chatham today!"

* Note on Winston Churchill's visit to Birchington in May 1944:-

In the build up to the D. Day landings during early May of 1944, there were two separate operations set in motion. The one, called 'Operation Overlord' was the official one based around Southampton, while a second 'hoax' one, named 'Operation Fortitude', was based in Kent. 'Overlord' had its destination set as the Normandy Beaches, while 'Fortitude' was set to land in the Pas de Calais area, the shorter and more obvious route. The huge build up of tanks and equipment in the Thanet area was all designed to fool the enemy. Even Churchill's visit to Birchington and the surrounding towns was part of this great subterfuge.

Charles Field, as it looks today. During the war the grass was uncut and there was a hedge along its boundary with Dane Road.

Chapter 8

1945

Water-rats

The trenches the troops had dug were now deserted. All the time the soldiers were using them and we went along afterwards looking for cartridge cases, the trenches remained dry. Now they were a third full of water and water-rats began to make their homes in them, burrowing holes in the banks on each side. Brian, Peter and I, with our dog Peggy, a smooth-haired terrier, tried to catch them, using the pointed ends of angle-irons and throwing them like spears. The angle-irons were for keeping the barbed wire in place and we found surplus ones in the long grass. But for all our efforts, the rats were too quick, so we resigned ourselves to just watching them swimming about and going into their holes.

Canterbury

Mother took us three children by double decker bus to Canterbury, now that it seemed safer to do so. We were appalled at the state of the city after the firebombing of 1942/3. A lot of it was just rubble where the shops once stood, but some had somehow managed to escape. It was in one of these – a tearoom – that we were able to get a cup of tea, after queuing for a long time. After all this, we were cheered by the sight of the Cathedral, which was still intact. We heard that the Luftwaffe also wanted it left untouched, as it was a 'marker' for its bombers and fighters. We also heard that Hitler wanted it for 'when' he had conquered Britain!

Concrete pillars – demolition

Concrete pillars of approximately 3 feet square by 7-8 feet high had been erected one foot apart on the pavement above the promenade, as an anti-invasion blockade. Now the time had come to demolish them. I was allowed to watch as each pillar was drilled with a single hole at the bottom with a pneumatic drill, then a stick of gelignite was placed in the hole, packed all round, then wires fixed from the pillar to a plunger. I got between two pillars a safe distance away as the explosive blew out the base of each pillar. All that was left holding it up were the 1 foot steel reinforced prongs. These were soon cut with an oxyacetylene torch. I was amazed at the force of the blast – it blew

pieces of concrete right through the sun shelter opposite. Eventually, all that blasting almost demolished the shelter, which was made of wood. The pieces also went straight through its tiled roof. I realised that I was in some danger as the work progressed, so I made my way home between the pillars that had not yet been blasted.

V. E. Day

It seemed many a long year since we had been allowed to have a bonfire and fireworks, but with the danger of invasion gone and now Victory in Europe, we were told we could now make a bonfire. People had been returning to their homes in dribs and drabs, with a few coming down to Minnis Bay. Knowing how the Allies were advancing in Germany, we realised that it would only be a short time before victory, so we began preparing weeks before. We built a bonfire in the dip, but we needed a Guy to go on top. There were plenty of surplus army uniforms, so father, who had done some tailoring with his sisters, who were seamstresses in the 1920/30s, set about converting a British Army battledress into that of a German High Command. The soldiers were very helpful when we told them our plans, and amongst other things, they produced a peaked cap. We used a pair of gloves for his hands. My father, who was artistic, made the head and face. When he had finished, we had a life-like "Hitler"! We were

A summer's day in our back garden, c.1943

A Street Party held in Lincoln Gardens near its corner with Rutland Gardens on 12th May 1945, kindly lent by Neil Somerford, who shared in the fun.

proud of our efforts and paraded it round on top of the pram. Owen, being the eldest, was in charge, as Brian, Peter, my sister and I went round knocking on people's doors. We had a mixed reception when we asked for "A penny for the Guy". One lady remarked, "Don't bring him in my house!" – referring to Hitler – while another set her dog on us! We thought that was not a very nice thing to do, but it was soon forgotten when the time came to light the bonfire. All explosive material was obviously used in munitions, so we knew there would be no fireworks. After putting the guy on top, we lit the fire. What we did not know was that this was a signal.

Suddenly, all the troops in the vicinity had surrounded us and joined in the merriment by throwing live blank .303 cartridges into the fire and letting off

Us in the back garden soo after the war

thunder-flashes. We were very close to where they exploded – it was deafening – but we did not mind. The soldiers had provided the 'fireworks', to our great delight. Everyone was happy singing songs and then a huge cheer went up when 'Hitler' caught fire and went up in a sheet of flames.

Peace in the Far East

Owen was at work in the locomotive sheds at Ramsgate by August, when peace in the Far East was announced. Without hesitation, all the footplate men jumped into the cabs of all the engines in steam and sounded their whistles – it could be heard all over the town!

In the next row of houses in our road, near where Brian lived, two ladies had moved in. One had an oriental look about her, perhaps Chinese, so father nicknamed her "Shanghai Lil". She had just given birth to a baby, whose father was one of the soldiers. Mother was invited along to see the baby. We three children did not remember seeing a newborn baby before, so went with mother to visit the infant – it was so tiny!

Back to normal?

At long last, we could now sleep in our own beds. It seemed strange and took us a long while to adapt. We could now use the front room again. We kept feeling that we should not be doing certain things and sometimes we would go back to sleeping on a mattress on the floor under the kitchen table again. It seemed unreal that we were going to resume a normal life, but it was good to see the joy on the faces of Mum and Dad, after the continuous strain of these last six years.

52

My family, taken at our house in Ethelbert Road, with our dog Peggy.

Derek in 1947

The Hart family on the sea defences in 1951

Postscript

Derek Hart finished his book without telling his readers very much about his life after the war. As I have been talking to local people about his story, many of them have commented on this fact, and asked if a few words could be added to complete his story.

After the war, Derek, Owen and their sister Pam continued to live in Ethelbert Road at Minnis Bay. During his childhood, Derek had always suffered with asthma, which was the reason he visited Great Ormond Street Hospital during the Blitz. Derek left school at the age of 16 in about 1950. He would have liked to join his brother Owen on the railway, but his mother felt that he would be better joining the Post Office. So he joined this Civil Service in 1951. If the family's finances had been greater, his own second choice (and possibly his father's choice for him, too) would have been the world of art. He continued to paint for the rest of his life. His greatest enjoyment came from painting in oils, but he also worked with watercolours quite skilfully. His favourite subject was the railway, which was an abiding passion from his earliest childhood, as readers will have realised. His model railway, which occupied a large area of one of his spare bedrooms, was carefully modelled on Birchington Station. As with everything he did, it was meticulously constructed, with every detail correctly placed.

Almost as soon as he left school his great enjoyment of cycling led him to join the Thanet Road Club, and he was a staunch member of this until the day he died. He was, in fact, returning from a rally at Reculver, when he had his fatal heart attack as he cycled home along the sea wall on 28th May 2003.

As soon as Derek reached 18 he did his National Service in the Royal Artillery as a Regimental Signaller. He had thought of following Owen's National Service choice into the R.A.F., but to do that he needed to sign on for three years, which he preferred not to do. On his return to civvy street, he went straight back into the Post Office, where he remained until he retired at 58 in 1991. During that time, he progressed from postman to driver and then to supervisor for the last twenty years of his service. When he retired after 41 years of service, (triggered by the Post Office making a very good offer to people like himself with over 40 years of service) he was able to devote the next four years to writing and researching his book. He was meticulous

in checking all his references and would lay out the various sections on which he was working over the floor around him. His wife commented that he looked as if he was marooned in a sea of papers.

Derek and Maureen met through the Thanet Road Club, Maureen having joined during his National Service time. They married on 3rd October 1959, setting up home eventually in Westgate. Their son Jason was born in 1969, followed three years later by Justin. From a very early age, they both became involved in family trips all over England in search of steam railway sites. Derek's other abiding interest was photography, but again, the slant was towards recording railway memorabilia.

After Derek's sudden death, his widow and sons all felt that it was a pity that his book had not been published and so Maureen approached the Birchington Heritage Trust, with a view to trying to achieve this. They felt it would be a fitting tribute to a dear husband and father. It would also give local people an insight into an era that many local children, who were evacuated, had missed. Added to this, it would give the present generation a new slant on childhood in the village between 1939-1945. Finally, newcomers to the village would be able to see something of the drama that now lies hidden beneath fifty years of peace.

Jennie Burgess

Executive Member of the Birchington Heritage Trust and Parish Archivist

Derek Hart had been a member of Thanet Road Club since the early 50s and had set a number of major club records

Cyclist in team which set club's 100-mile record

A DEDICATED Thanet cyclist has died after a heart attack. Derek Hart had been watching a club event and set off along the sea wall from Reculver to cycle to his home in Westgate when he became ill.

He was found by two girls on the beach half-a-mile from Reculver towers and taken to Canterbury hospital where he was pronounced dead.

Mr Hart had been a member of Thanet Road Club since the early 50s.

His best times were set between 1957 and 1964. During this period he was a member of the Thanet team that won the 1961 Medway Wheelers Roy Enfield Memorial 50 in a time of six hours, 22 minutes, 45 seconds.

He was also in the team with Brian Doherty and Stan Clements that set a club 100-mile team record of 13 hours, 45 minutes, 52 seconds in 1957.

Thanet Road Club president Dave Saffery said: "Derek was one of the few people who could recall times done by various riders in time trials and competition records from many years back. Many members of the club will sorely miss him."

Mr Hart, who lived in Westgate Bay Avenue, started out as a messenger boy after leaving school and spent all his working life with the postal service.

He spent his two-year period of national service with the national artillery on Sheppey.

He was 68 and leaves a widow, Maureen, and two sons.

Index